Social Media, Organizational Identity and Public Relations

T0330835

Public relations has been swift to grasp social media, yet its impact on public relations practice remains relatively unexplored. This book focusses on a way of understanding organizational identity construction in a virtual context, developing scholarship on the importance of a virtual presence in PR management, and further, to make sense of these identities as authentic, legitimate or plausible.

Through a diverse group of empirical case studies, this book explores the global perspective on organizational identities which transcend global boundaries via the internet including Volkswagen's emissions scandal and Monsanto and organized social media protests. It also explores crowdfunding – an emerging form of capitalist development constructed through sensemaking in social media. By looking at the emergence of organization in today's social media environment, it identifies how the interactive is created on a digitally mediated platform, sharing knowledge and engaging individuals in organizational identity construction.

Viewing the social construction of organizational identities through this lens, this innovative book locates how identities are plausible, authentic and legitimate – or not – through their ongoing communication via social media. It will be of great interest to academics teaching and researching in public relations, organizational communication and social media.

Amy Thurlow is Professor of Communication Studies at Mount Saint Vincent University in Halifax, Canada where she teaches public relations and organizational communication. Her recent publications appear in *Qualitative Research in Organizations and Management, The Scandinavian Journal of Management, Journal of Change Management* and the *Canadian Journal of Communication*. Currently, she is a co-investigator on a five-year, multi-institutional SSHRC funded project focused on *Reassembling Canadian Management Knowledge* with a special interest in dispersion, equity, identity and history. She is a member of the National Education Council of the Canadian Public Relations Society and the international Commission on Public Relations Education.

Social Media, Organizational Identity and Public Relations

The Challenge of Authenticity

Amy Thurlow

LONDON AND NEW YORK

First published 2019
by Routledge
2 Park Square, Milton Park, Abingdon, Oxon OX14 4RN

and by Routledge
52 Vanderbilt Avenue, New York, NY 10017

First issued in paperback 2020

Routledge is an imprint of the Taylor & Francis Group, an informa business

British Library Cataloguing-in-Publication Data
A catalogue record for this book is available from the British Library

Library of Congress Cataloging-in-Publication Data
Names: Thurlow, Amy, author.
Title: Social media, organizational identity and public relations : the
    challenge of authenticity / Amy Thurlow.
Description: 1 Edition. | New York : Routledge, 2019. | Includes
    bibliographical references and index. |
Identifiers: LCCN 2018030478 (print) | LCCN 2018032116 (ebook) |
    ISBN 9781315160443 (ebook) | ISBN 9781138064324
    (hardback : alk. paper)
Subjects: LCSH: Public relations. | Social media. | Organizational
    behavior.
Classification: LCC HD59 (ebook) | LCC HD59 .T487 2019 (print) |
    DDC 659.20285/4678—dc23
LC record available at https://lccn.loc.gov/2018030478

ISBN 13: 978-0-367-66503-6 (pbk)
ISBN 13: 978-1-138-06432-4 (hbk)

Typeset in Sabon
by Apex CoVantage, LLC

To my husband Paul Card for always believing in me, to my mother Dana Thurlow for her encouragement and support, and to my children Mirissa and Owen Card for their love and hugs.

Contents

Acknowledgments   viii

1 Introduction   1

2 Communicatively constituted organizations,
  plausible?   8

3 Critical Sensemaking (CSM) in a virtual environment   22

4 Methodology   36

5 Plausibility, authenticity and collective enactment   43

6 Crowdfunding – collective organizing and virtual
  identities   57

7 Plausibility and legitimation   66

8 Volkswagen – truth, accuracy and plausibility   78

9 Engagement and enactment   85

10 #MarchAgainstMonsanto – social movements,
   extracting cues and the ongoing nature of
   sensemaking   98

11 Conclusion   104

References   111
Index   127

Acknowledgments

Thank-you to my research mentors and friends Dr. Jean Helms Mills and Dr. Albert Mills for their guidance, teaching and encouragement.

1 Introduction

Social media construct a reality where networks, artifacts, actors, meanings and identities converge without the traditional limitations of time and space (Gilpin, Palazzolo, & Brody, 2010; Fuchs, 2005). The volume of information available through this media, its persistence and its frenzied nature create a challenging landscape for communicators concerned with authenticity and organizational identity.

Over the past two decades, the literature on organizational identity has expanded, changed and required researchers to explore how, and by whom, identities are constructed. Within this research, essentially two main perspectives are presented on the nature of identity. Traditionally, the organizational literature has held that identity is a relatively fixed element (Albert & Whetten, 1985). In that vein, Gagliardi (1986) argued that the primary strategy of an organization is to maintain its identity and that organizations change, in actual fact, only to preserve the essence of their identities. However, in their study of sensemaking during strategic change, Gioia and Thomas (1996) challenged this perspective. They questioned the previously held assumption that identity has permanency in organizations and individuals, and suggest that the concept of identity "may be more fluid than the organizational literature has suggested" (Gioia & Thomas, 1996, p. 371). In fact, this perspective suggests that organizations have multiple identities, in multiple contexts with multiple audiences (Gioia, Schultz, & Corley, 2000). This social constructivist approach has opened the door to many more questions about how individuals within organizations make sense of changing identities.

More recently, the changing nature of digital media communication has demanded that public relations scholars investigate organizational identity in a dynamic and emerging social media context (Dawson, 2015). The further question of how individuals and organizations make sense of these identities is equally important. Let's take as a starting point the contention put forward by Weick, Sutcliff, and Obsfeld (2005, p. 416) that, "who we are lies importantly in the hands of others, which means our categories for sensemaking lie in their hands. If their images of us change, our identities may be destabilized and our receptiveness to new meanings increases."

From there, Weick et al. (2005) go on to explain the fluidity of individual identities in sensemaking terms saying, "Identity [may] turn out to be an issue of plausibility rather than accuracy, just as is the case for many issues that involve organizing and sensemaking" (p. 416).

Viewing the social construction of organizational identities through this lens, this book will investigate examples of identities that have been made sense of as plausible, authentic and legitimate, or not, in their ongoing communication through social media platforms. This first chapter will introduce the groundwork for the critical analysis of meanings constructed as authentic. The contention here is that social media interactions produce not only channels of and traces of communication, but artifacts of that communication as well. Through the textual production of discursive communication in the form of tweets, posts, shares and likes, individuals collectively construct a socially mediated identity of the organizations with which they are associated. Ultimately, as Putnam and Cooren (2004, p. 323) suggest, discourse "is more than an artifact or a reflection of an organization; rather it forms the foundation for organizing and for developing the notion of organization as an entity." Social media is also a particularly interesting site of inquiry as it is a contested space in which identity may be both constructed and deconstructed. As Albu and Etter (2016, p. 8) point out, "instead of creating stable structures for information dissemination, social media technologies are volatile and performative and may cause unintended consequences."

This is not to say, however, that the identities of organizations within social media should be separated from the context of their representations in the offline world. Or that these identities are distinct simply because they occur within the bounds of a particular technology. Meanings constructed within a social media context are understood here to emerge from a particular context, through identified channels, and within a broader communicative environment. As Jurgenson (2012) refers "to a larger conceptual perspective that views our reality as the byproduct of the enmeshing of the on and offline" (p. 84), our understandings of identity constructed within social media must reflect elements of the broader communication environment as well. Jurgenson (2012, p. 84) cautions against separating these dimensions within a form of 'digital dualism' which isolates online communication from the rest of the communicative context. As Unger, Wodak, and Khosravinik (2016) conclude, any text may be seen as existing within multiple contexts. In that sense I will not separate online and offline communication as independent of one another, but simply as representing particular elements of a shared broader context. This includes a context wherein content and users from different sources are publicly associated in indiscriminate and unforeseen ways (Albu & Etter, 2016). My intention here is to locate the constitution of organization through social media within broader processes of sensemaking.

I have been using the term *social media* so far in this introduction to identify a particular technological manner of communication, with its own distinctive characteristics in regard to the construction of meaning, identity and network. At the same time, I am aware that there is no consensus within the literature on exactly what the category of social media defines, nor as to how social media is used. As a starting point, I am using Kaplan and Haenlein's (2010) definition of social media as "a group of internet-based applications that build on the ideological and technological foundations of Web 2.0, and that allow the creation and exchange of user generated content" (p. 61). As they further point out, however, the broad term of social media has been applied to a wide variety of technologies which are rapidly emerging, converging and re-imaging themselves in a dynamic technological environment (Kaplan & Haenlein, 2010).

Kane, Alavi, Labianca, and Borgatti (2014) also make the point that it may be difficult to clarify what is technologically distinctive about technologies currently labeled as social media because in some cases they reflect characteristics of prior collaborative technologies that introduced knowledge management systems or group decision support systems (Butler, 2001; & Poole, 1994; Alavi & Leidner, 2001) prior to the advent of digital media technologies (Kane et al., 2014).

A third challenge in defining social media is the behavioral impact of individual technologies. As Kane et al. caution,

> Even though many of the technological distinctions enacted by social media may only be a matter of degree, the rapid adoption and widespread use of these tools mean that even relatively minor technological differences may result in profound theoretical consequences for individual and organizational behavior.
>
> (2014, p. 276)

That being said, there are some common elements to the nature and uses of social media, as identified in Boyd and Ellison's (2007, p. 2) definition of social networking sites,

> We define social network sites as web-based services that allow individuals to (1) construct a public or semi-public profile within a bounded system, (2) articulate a list of other users with whom they share a connection, and (3) view and traverse their list of connections and those made by others within the system. The nature and nomenclature of these connections may vary from site to site.

With these commonalities and differences in mind, I proceed in the direction that Leclercq-Vandelannoitte (2011, p. 1267) articulates as she summarizes Foucault's argument, "it is not so much the technological instruments but the discursive practices and power relations that surround them, together with the knowledge and behavior they produce, that matters." To that end, I will draw on the conceptual framework of *communication as constitutive of organization* (CCO). CCO theory identifies communication as the 'building block' of organizations (Christensen & Cornelissen, 2011, p. 398). Theorists in this tradition have built on Weick's (1979) work on sensemaking and the process of organizing, to develop a perspective which situates communication as the central, constitutive force in organizing and thus organizations. Although the specific approaches within the theory of CCO may vary (Ashcraft, Kuhn, & Cooren, 2009; Putnam & Nicotera, 2010), there is a common focus on the centrality of language, speech, text and discourse to collective sensemaking within organizations. As Putnam and Nicotera (2009, p. 482) summarize, "CCO is first and foremost a collection of perspectives about grounding the role of communication in the ontology of an organization." Koschmann (2013, p. 65) summarizes the constitutive approach as seeing "communication as generative of organizational realities and the fundamental process by which we know and understand the social world."

In their overview of the contributions of CCO theory, Cooren, Kuhn, Cornelissen, and Clark (2011) indicate the importance of CCO scholarship to the existing and growing research on organizational identity. Cooren et al. (2011, p. 1159) point out that CCO provides a valuable perspective on organizational identity and "connects with recent interests in organizational identity from a discourse perspective" (i.e. Leclercq-Vandelannoitte, 2011). From this perspective CCO and current work on discourse and identity continue to reflect organizations as "socially constructed from networks of conversations or dialogues" (Humphreys & Brown, 2002, p. 422).

Cooren and Taylor (1997) have laid the groundwork for further understandings of organizational identity as existing only as "discourse where its reality is created, and sustained" (p. 429). Following from this perspective, further work from these scholars and others in the CCO paradigm have expanded theory on the communicatively constituted nature of organizations to address ways in which individual voices may connect to broader, organizational perspectives. These processes may be embedded or productive of organizational rules and procedures that amplify the power of individual voices and shape future actions and meanings (Taylor & Van Every, 2000).

To gain further insight into the individual and collective processes of identity construction through social media, I also employ here the analytic framework of Critical Sensemaking (CSM) (Helms Mills, Thurlow & Mills, 2010; Helms Mills, 2003). Using this layered approach allows for a more thorough understanding of CCO and CSM and how these two perspectives can work together. For instance, one of the limitations of the CCO perspective is that it does not fully deal with the issue of power. Critical Sensemaking allows for a more fulsome investigation of the power structures at work in processes of organizing and organization which serve to constrain the range of plausible identities available to individuals as they co-construct shared meaning.

As a critical framework and method, Critical Sensemaking (CSM) offers great potential as a theoretical framework for understanding the complex relationships between organizations, identities and social media within a communicatively constituted context. Identity construction as a process represents a growing literature, both in the organizational studies and communication studies disciplines. However, the advent of social media technologies, and the impact that these technologies have had on communicative processes, have transformed the ways in which identities are constructed, and challenge researchers to develop new understandings of how communication, discourse, technology and organization come together.

CSM starts with Weick's (1995) psycho-social properties of sensemaking which tell us that sensemaking is (1) grounded in identity construction, (2) retrospective, (3) enactive of sensible environments, (4) social, (5) ongoing, (6) focused on and by extracted cues and (7) driven by plausibility rather than accuracy. However, these properties on their own do not fully explain why some experiences, language and events become meaningful for individuals while others do not (Helms Mills, 2003; Helms Mills, Thurlow, & Mills, 2010). Individuals do not make sense of their experiences in isolation from their broader environments. CSM is primarily concerned with ways in which individuals make sense of their complex environments. It puts sensemaking in context by surfacing issues of power and privilege in the process of understanding why some language, social practices and identities become meaningful for individuals while others do not (Thurlow, 2010).

These two perspectives, CCO and CSM, converge to inform our understandings of how communication is made 'real,' in this case, in terms of identity. Taylor (1999) points out that, "organization emerges in communication as the consequence of a mapping of the interactive, or 'conversational,' dimension onto the textual in order to produce organization as (1) knowledge shared by its members and (2) activity in which they are engaged" (p. 24).

The emergence of organization in today's social media environment demonstrates how the interactive is created as real on a digitally mediated platform which at the same time shares knowledge among members and engages individuals in the activity of organizational identity construction. This understanding of identity challenges the dominant management contention that organizational identity is a strategic tool for building credibility and increasing profitability and influence among stakeholders (cf. Dowling, 1986) and emphasizes what McNamara and Zerfass suggest, that social media in organizational communication is "mostly experimental and ad hoc, rather than strategically planned" (McNamara & Zerfass, 2012, p. 303). Although much has been written on the importance of a virtual presence in organizational management (Khang, Ki, & Ye, 2012), there has been relatively little scholarship on how to make sense of these identities as authentic, legitimate or plausible.

Clearly, the literature on social media and organizational identity presents us with a complex set of questions in a constantly changing environment. In this volume, I will attempt to address three of the key themes that emerge from the literature. The first is the work on critical understandings of the process of sensemaking in the construction of virtual identities, the second theme deals with authenticity, plausibility and legitimation in mediated identity construction, and the third theme is concerned with communicatively constituted organizational identities in a social media context.

By selecting a diverse group of case study organizations, the focus of this book offers a global perspective on identities which transcend national boundaries via the internet. The featured organizations will include; Volkswagen, specifically with regard to the recent environmental emissions scandal; Monsanto, in relation to the organized social media movement March against Monsanto; and a group of smaller case studies on crowdfunding – an emerging form of capitalist development constructed through sensemaking in social media. The crowdfunding initiatives will reflect organizations from the health care sector as well as social justice projects.

Chapters 1–4 provide an introduction to the core questions of identity construction and the main perspectives discussed in this book, communication as constitutive of organization theory and the analytic framework of critical sensemaking. Chapters 5 and 6 turn their focus to the question of discursive power and legitimation, and begin to look at examples of identity construction in organizational context. Chapter 5 addresses the question of discursive power as reflected in the rhetorical strategies and practices of organizations in the process of constructing their identities. Chapter 6 is titled, Crowdfunding – collective organizing and virtual identities. This chapter presents several empirical examples as a series of discussions to illustrate the discourse of capitalism and the process of identity construction converging on social media platforms.

Chapters 7 and 8 investigate social media identities in crisis. Chapter 7, titled *Plausibility and legitimation*, analyzes intersections within these two processes. In these intersections we are able to see points of connection in the sensemaking process whereby the property of plausibility is strengthened in relation to other properties with the introduction of various legitimation strategies. Chapter 8, entitled *Volkswagen – truth, accuracy and plausibility*, follows with a deconstruction of text surrounding that organization's emissions control scandal. This analysis uses a Critical Sensemaking framework to analyze the documentation of the scandal across social media.

Chapters 9 to 11 offer some insights into the process of actively engaging in sensemaking and identity, leading to some suggestions for further study and questions about the future of technology, identity and communication. Chapter 9, *Engagement and enactment*, provides a discussion of the process of sensemaking as evidenced in one of the core properties within that process, enactment. In this chapter, I discuss the nature of enactment from within the sensemaking framework, highlighting the ways that meaning and identity are constructed through the actions (including language and text) of the sensemakers themselves. This form of active sensemaking coincides with the propensity toward user engagement which characterizes social media platforms.

Chapter 10, *#MarchAgainstMonsanto – social movements, extracting cues and the ongoing nature of sensemaking*, explores enactment further. This chapter explores mobilization of social movements via social media from a Critical Sensemaking perspective. In the example of this controversial social initiative, #MarchAgainsMonsanto, the organizational identity of a multinational corporation is challenged by an emerging identity constructed through social interaction. Of particular interest within this process is the crafting of narratives that construct meanings around engagement and enactment, while at the same time highlighting cues from a complex communication environment. The text analyzed in this chapter reflects both narrative data at a particular point in time, as well as an ongoing conversation or narrative construction as key influencers in the social media networks enroll individuals into their social media network and enlarge the reach and range of messages. At the same time, the messages themselves evolve and are re-constituted or co-constituted as they are shared and re-tweeted to the network.

Finally, Chapter 11 pulls together key themes in the book and highlights insights from the featured cases. By investigating the identities which emerge as narratives from the interactive communication networks featured here, I offer some concluding thoughts on how both the process of sensemaking and the communicatively constituted nature of organizations converge on social media, and suggest some further questions regarding technology, identity and communication.

2 Communicatively constituted organizations, plausible?

To further explore the relationships between organization and identity, in this chapter I provide an overview of the CCO perspective. In doing so I identify the ways in which understandings of organizations and organizational events as communicatively constituted can inform individual engagement in processes of organizing. From that perspective, I suggest that organizational identities which emerge as durable and persist within and beyond the organization are created and maintained in language, not actions or results (Grant, Keenoy, & Oswick, 1998). Thus, a company's identity may be formed with rhetoric, not tangible results of management processes (Oswick, Grant, Michelson, & Wailes, 2005; Thurlow & Mills, 2009).

Although conceptualizations of organizations as communicatively constituted are gaining momentum and reach in the literature, methodological applications and frameworks of analysis to operationalize this perspective are still somewhat limited. To date, "the CCO perspective's range of methodologies is still limited to analyzing local communication episodes, rather than studying organizations as broader networks of communication episodes" (Blaschke, Schoeneborn, & Seidl, 2012, p. 879). Tackling the broader questions of networked identities is a difficult one, and from a CCO perspective this may take one of several different approaches. Throughout this volume the term CCO will represent the phrase *communication is constitutive of organizing* (Putnam & Nicotera, 2009). Bisel (2010) describes the current state of CCO quite succinctly when he says, "CCO theories articulate a communicative ontology of organization. Although the specific mechanisms and processes by which communication is associated with organization are debated hotly among theorists, one premise remains constant across the tradition: Communication calls organization into being" (Bisel, 2010, p. 124).

This statement emphasizes the fact that even though the specific approaches within the CCO approach may vary (Ashcraft et al., 2009; Putnam & Nicotera, 2009), there is a common focus on the centrality of language, speech, text and discourse to collective sensemaking within organizations. As Putnam and Nicotera (2009) summarize, "CCO is first and foremost a collection of perspectives about grounding the role of communication in the ontology of an organization" (p 482). They further describe the central focus of CCO as "a body of work connected by a central question or an overall problem rather than a clear-cut answer" (Putnam & Nicotera, 2010, p. 158). Schoeneborn and Vasquez (2017) further summarize the body of work as "based on the idea that organization emerges in and is sustained and transformed by communication" (p. 367). And Koschmann (2013, p. 65) contributes to the definition of CCO, describing it as a constitutive approach which views "communication as generative of organizational realities and the fundamental process by which we know and understand the social world."

Within the family of theories which collectively represent CCO theory, there are essentially three distinct schools of thought. However, as Schoeneborn et al. (2014, p. 305) summarize,

> the strongest commonality among the three schools . . . is the presumed link between organization and communication. All three schools are fundamentally grounded in the assumption that the organization does not pre-date communication but emerges and perpetuates itself as a network of interlocking communication events (Blaschke et al., 2012; Taylor & Van Every, 2000) or flows (McPhee & Zaug, 2000).

Tackling the central question identified through CCO has been the focus of multiple approaches. Ideas about how organizations emerge through communicative processes are surfaced throughout the organizational identity literature over the past several decades, but the early work in CCO originates in 2000 when two of the three dominant perspectives within this tradition were presented. In that year, Taylor and Van Every published their trail-blazing book entitled, The Emergent Organization: Communication as its Site and Surface (Taylor & Van Every, 2000). In the book's preface the authors introduce that work as "the culmination of a long quest: to explain organization in the language of an authentically communicational theory" (Taylor & Van Every, 2000, p. ix). And that same year, McPhee and Zaug published their innovative article, The Communicative Constitution of Organizations: A Framework for Explanation (McPhee & Zaug, 2000). While both of these works are recognized now as foundational to the establishment of the CCO literature, they offered different approaches to understanding how communication and organization are interconnected in their production. And ultimately, scholarship emerging from this point of origin can be broken into three distinctive schools of thought known generally as: The Montreal School, The Four Flows Approach and Luhmann's Theory of Social Systems.

Taylor and Van Emery's (2000) book is a defining work of what has evolved as the Montreal School of organizational communication. They argue that organizations emanate from two communicative circumstances, 'conversation' and 'text.' Text is understood as a structuring principle which can include any 'stable patterning' or documenting of values, roles or rules which govern the organizational identity. In contrast, 'conversation' is seen as the shared interactions occurring in everyday situations when people come together to coordinate around specific objectives (p. 35). These interactions can be recorded or fixed in texts that contribute to the persistence and durability of the organizational identity. Text can be represented in a multitude of forms including, for example, the architecture of buildings, organizational documents, technologies and processes (Cooren & Fairhurst, 2009). Further, from this perspective, text and conversation are seen to co-constitute each other and together they form 'a self-organizing loop' (Taylor & Van Every, 2000). Fairhurst and Putnam (2004) highlight the potential of this self-organizing loop in terms of sites that could capture the constitutive nature of both text and conversation as social practices and as enduring systems of thought at a particular point in time.

McPhee and Zaug (2000) introduced the Four Flows approach, predicated on four communication flows: activity coordination, self-structuring, membership negotiation and institutional positioning, within their understanding of communicative organizations. Activity coordination was described as a flow that encompassed connections between work practices as produced through rhetorical and discursive power. Organizational self-structuring was concerned with structures that set boundaries around and within the organization and informed strategic direction. Membership negotiation was a flow of practices related to relationship formation, network building and inclusion, or exclusion of organizational members. And Institutional positioning focused on external as well as internal stakeholders to address the ways in which organizations position themselves relative to other organizations and society. As Bisel (2010) explains, these four flows are located

> among the microlevel talk of instructions and commands (i.e., activity coordination), the macrolevel talk about how the organization should function and what image it should attempt to create (i.e., self-structuring and institutional positioning, respectively), and the mesolevel talk of culture and socialization (i.e., membership negotiation).
>
> (Bisel, 2010, p. 126)

In Schoeneborn et al. (2014, p. 291), Robert McPhee describes the understanding of communication reflected in the Four Flows approach as a process of

> symbolic transtruction, where 'transtruction' means the intermediation of each of four basic dimensions of action – signification, domination, legitimation and constitution (see McPhee, 1998) – by the other three dimensions. In other words, communication is the fused emergence, in symbolic interaction, of meaning – in the first instance, as we are

talking about communication – power, and its bases; normative force, and socially or materially constituted systems and contexts.

McPhee continues on to emphasize the usefulness of all four dimensions as they "elaborate the complexity" (in Schoeneborn et al., 2014, p. 291) that communication involves.

This approach has been adopted by CCO scholars interested in understanding the organization as a reflection of rules and structures that are used by individuals within organizations to guide their social interactions (for example, McPhee & Iverson, 2009); Browning, Greene, Sitkin, Sutcliffe, & Obstfeld, 2009). With a strong focus on organizational and social structures, essentially the Four Flows approach is rooted in Giddens' (1979, 1984) view of structure (Structuration Theory). McPhee and Zaug (2000) posited that organizations emerge from the four processes above which structured how individuals organized and created organizations. McPhee (Schoeneborn et al., 2014, p. 294) reaffirms that connection to Giddens' work as he accepts Gidden's (1984) definition of organization as "collectivities in which the reflexive regulation of the conditions of system reproduction looms large in the continuity of day-to-day practices" (p. 200). This definition differs from that of the Montreal School in terms of the focus on structure. For example, boundaries around membership would be well defined and their permeability determined and communicated.

The Four Flows approach has been critiqued for its focus on structure, as well as on the application of the flows individually (Bisel, 2010; Sillince, 2010). Perhaps the strongest critiques are around the definition of organization. However, Putnam and Nicotera (2010) in their response to questions about CCO theory assert that

> For McPhee and Zaug, an organization exists in time and space as a texture of practice in which the four flows are interwoven, like hues of yarn that become inextricably intertwined and in combination constitute a new form. Treating the flows as a texture of practices envisions any one of them as a prototype rather than a necessary and sufficient condition of an organization.
>
> (p. 4)

This description of the approach as an overall tapestry as opposed to a rigid application of process does perhaps open the door to a broader integration of aspects of this model with the other two perspectives.

The third approach to CCO is referred to as Luhmann's Theory of Social Systems. Brummans, Cooren, Robichaud, and Taylor (2014) describe this perspective as an emerging approach to CCO, reflecting an understanding of the relationship between communication and organizing as a process of self-referential systems. The social systems approach draws from Luhman's

(1992, 1995) foundational work on Social Systems Theory and emphasizes the systems-level processes which engage communication in organizing. From this perspective Luhman saw communication as a critical component in the building of and functioning of social systems. As quoted in Brummans et al. (2014, p. 185), Luhman (1995) explains that

> in social systems formed by communication, only communication is available as a means of decomposing elements. . . . A social system has no other manner of dissection; it cannot resort to chemical, neurophysiological, or mental processes (although all these exist and play a part). In other words, one cannot bypass the constitutive level of communication.
>
> (p. 164)

In Schoeneborn et al. (2014), CCO scholar David Seidl describes Luhmann's perspective on communication as a

> purely social phenomenon. In this sense, communication has to be conceptualized as an emergent phenomenon that arises from the interaction between individuals. Extending this line of reasoning, Luhmann argues that what matters is not how a particular individual understands a communication but how a subsequent communication interprets the preceding communication it is connected to; only a communicative event can determine the particular way in which the immediately preceding communicative event is understood. For example, from a given answer, you can infer how the respective question has been understood.
>
> (290–291)

In this sense, Luhmann (1995) suggests that communication can only be understood, or made possible, retrospectively.

In contrast to the Montreal School approach, however, Luhmann uses the term organization in a much narrower sense. As Seidl (Schoeneborn et al., 2014, p. 293) explains,

> For Luhmann (2003), organizations are one of three generic types of social systems; the other two being society (i.e. the system encompassing all communication) and face to face interactions (i.e. the system encompassing communication between people who reflexively perceive each other as present. All three types of social systems are conceptualized as 'autopoietic' (i.e. self-reproducing) communication systems that are able to process meaning.

Although I have discussed three somewhat distinctive orientations of the CCO approach, the strong commonalities in the foundational assumptions of CCO mean that these may not necessarily be mutually exclusive ways of seeing organizations and identity. The foundational element in each of these perspectives, of course, reflects the formative nature of language and communication. And, as Putnam and Fairhurst (2015) suggest, each of these three understandings had weaknesses that could be addressed by the other two perspectives. They further advocate that theory building should cross perspectives, and encourage the potential in "using the object orientation to address relativism in the becoming approach as well as introducing materiality in the grounded-in-action view" (Putnam & Fairhurst, 2015, p. 377).

The CCO perspective adopted in this book is, for the most part, that of the Montreal School approach. Although, as suggested previously, elements of the other two schools of thought are certainly reflected in the chapters that follow. For an analysis of identity construction in social media, the Montreal School appealed to me largely for its compatibility with other discursive approaches which offered insights into this question. In his interview at the Hamburg panel discussion on CCO thinking facilitated by Dennis Schoeneborn, Montreal School scholar Francois Cooren indicated that the epistemological foundations of this stream of CCO theory are relational (Schoeneborn et al., 2014):

> By relational epistemology, I mean the kind of epistemology that was put forward by pragmatist scholars such as Charles Sanders Peirce, John Dewey and, to a lesser extent William James. A relational or pragmatist epistemology calls into question both subjectivism and idealism, on one hand, and empiricism and materialism on the other by refusing to determine a starting point in the act of knowing, inquiring or investigating.
>
> (p. 288)

This orientation allows for deep connections with other approaches which support both critical sensemaking and organizational communication such as Actor Network Theory (Latour, 2005, 2013) and Framing Theory (Entman, 1993). Perhaps most importantly for the purposes this research, The Montreal School approach also allows for the investigation of synergies between the Critical Sensemaking framework and elements of CCO as they relate to identity construction, plausibility and enactment in the creation of meaning. These synergies reflect complementary approaches, enhancing the usefulness of both frameworks for research on the diverse landscape of social media. For example, the position of the Montreal School approach in refusing to determine a starting point in the communication process is balanced by the CSM position of bracketing a sensemaking process which begins with a shock and ends with the restoration of routine or establishment of order. Although these positions may appear incompatible at first, they actually serve to highlight both the ongoing and retrospective elements of sensemaking (which transcend the brackets) and the constant flux of the social media landscape, which is ultimately an ongoing process as opposed to a distinct conversation. Of course, elements of the other two

CCO approaches may also come into play here, indicating other points at which to investigate an 'act of knowing, inquiry or investigation.' Luhman's Theory of Social Systems approach, for instance, firmly determines a starting point of communication, that of the observer "a human being, a social system (e.g. an organization), or even a machine – and the observations (see Seidl & Becker, 2006)" (Schoeneborn et al., 2014, p. 288). This approach is interested in the ways in which an observer may structure observations and ultimately construct reality within this process. Insights from this approach may be useful in understanding how particular sensemaking occurs from a retrospective point of view, for example.

Although there may be differences in interpretation about where sensemaking starts, both the Montreal School view of CCO and CSM are in agreement that action is central to communication. Weick (1995) clearly identifies enactment as the property which brings sensemaking into being, with action being defined quite broadly in terms of the production and enactment of text and discourse. Similarly, the Montreal School view of CCO tends to define communication in terms of enactment. As Cooren explains, "communication is, first and foremost, considered an action" (Schoeneborn et al., 2014, p. 289).

Another appealing feature of this interpretation of CCO is the view that communication involves not just humans, but other entities as well. This view is incorporated into CSM through the element of formative context, and also central to Actor Network Theory in the description of non-human actants operating within and upon networks. Cooren explains that

> communication should not be considered an activity that only concerns human beings. Many other things get communicated through what people say, write or do: emotions, ideas, beliefs, values, positions, but also – and through the latter of these – situations, facts, realities and so on.
>
> (Schoeneborn et al., 2014, p. 290)

He continues on to explain that

> regarding the question of non-human agency, we see that, indeed, artifacts have a big role to play in the communicative constitution of an organization. They matter a lot. They count. They display agency to the extent that they . . . communicate how an organization is perceived and experienced – think of buildings, machines, and logos, for instance.
>
> (p. 298)

This perspective is particularly useful in an investigation of communication mediated through social media networks. Although we may not be talking about buildings here, there are certainly other elements of architecture in digital structures, such as website designs, which convey meaning. Likewise, the nature of social media allows for multi-platform sharing of not just textual elements, understood here in a broad sense (written, visual, iconic, ideational, oral, etc.), but also of discourse, and to that end, discursive practices. As Cooren (2004, p. 375) reminds us, "organizational activities, are discursively structured, which means that text in all its forms (written, oral, iconic) can display a form of agency" and he concludes, these texts can make a difference. This textual agency essentially takes place as soon as a text is produced and disseminated across the network. The moment that the text takes on agency is almost instantaneous now as by clicking a button, the content producer sends that text out into an 'uncontrolled' environment where it may be transformed, endorsed, refuted, etc., by other members of that network and beyond. It takes on its own being, and becomes in itself an artifact of organization.

The Montreal School perspective is also useful in terms of insights into how organizational membership may be understood. This element is critical in understanding social media networks, which are sites of constant and often contentious negotiated memberships. Dobusch and Schoeneborn (2015) address this question in their work on the communicative constitution of Anonymous, a controversial online organization of 'hacktivists' who conceal their identities as they conduct political or other social actions of resistance. Dobusch et al. (2015) categorize this group as part of an emergent form of organization which they characterize as resembling a looser social collective. Organizations in this category would include online communities (Garud, Jain, & Tuertscher, 2008; O'Mahony & Ferraro, 2007; Puranam, Alexy, & Reitzig, 2014), hacker collectives (Coleman, 2014; Scott, 2013) and terrorist networks (Comas, Shrivastava, & Martin, 2015; Schoeneborn & Scherer, 2012; Stohl & Stohl, 2011)" (p. 1005). According to Dobusch et al. (2015), what these organizations have in common is a fluidity of membership, boundaries and identity. This high degree of fluidity is typical of many online social networks and challenges some of the long-held assumptions of organization in more traditional organizational theory. Schreyogg and Sydow, 2010 (p. 1253) point out that traditionally organizations are "simply not conceivable without reference to workable identities and boundaries."

However, Dobusch et al. (2015) argue that this perspective fails to acknowledge that even highly fluid forms of organizing can 'gain the status of organizational entities and actors,' as in the case of Anonymous. They further point to the work of Tsoukas and Chia (2002) who call for a recognition of organizations as more than static entities but as ongoing processes of becoming. This approach fits as well with Weick's interpretation of organizations as process driven as opposed to structurally driven. Dobusch et al. (2015) further suggest that it is the advent of new digital technologies and the social networks that they invoke, such as open source software, wikis and social media, that make these new and more loosely characterized forms of organizing possible (e.g. Puranam et al., 2014).

Dobusch et al. (2015) draw on CCO theory to illuminate their work in this area because of the central idea in this perspective that

> organizations are not primarily comprised of their members or job roles but come into existence through the continuous layering of conversations and texts that become constantly interconnected and collectively evoke and stabilize the organization as an identifiable entity or actor (Taylor and Van Every, 2000, 2011; Cooren, 2010).
>
> (p. 1012)

They in particular draw on the insights within CCO theory concerned with communication as a dynamic "process of manipulating symbols toward the creation, maintenance, destruction, and/or transformation of meanings, which are axial – not peripheral – to organizational existence and organizing phenomena" (Ashcraft et al., 2009, p. 22). From within this perspective, fluid or loosely structured organizations can be included in analysis of organizational processes. From the perspective of the Four Flows school, Dobusch et al. (2015) take the position that membership negotiation is one of the central components of organization. This negotiation can be conducted through both human and non-human actants, and essentially requires decision making around the location of authority on behalf of the organization., i.e. who has the authority to speak or act on behalf of the organization. This negotiation is typical within many social media networks, and even formal organizations operating offline struggle with the need to 'control' access to textual production on behalf of the organization by individual members without that level of authority.

In their conclusion, Dobusch et al. (2015) indicate that organizationality (a term they propose to refer to the degree to which a social collective meets the requirements for organization) "is a precarious accomplishment (see Cooren et al., 2011) that needs to be repeatedly reinstated through the performance of certain speech acts (e.g. identity claims) and their attribution to an overarching organizational address (see also Drepper, 2005)" (p. 1030).

That is not to suggest that fluidity in organizational form and membership is limited to social media. Koschmann (2013) further illustrates the challenges of membership negotiation in his work on Interorganizational collaborations, concluding that one of the central barriers to establishing collective identity in organization is the negotiation and organization of members with competing values and interests. In his work, however, he draws on the Montreal School approach to discuss membership in relation to authority. Using this approach he describes authority as coming from "abstraction and reification" (p. 68). He continues to describe the process of distancing an author from the textual production and thereby re-enforcing agency within the text itself, not the individual. This process is called distanciation and as it continues and texts are further removed from their immediate circumstances, more and more ambiguity is introduced until all that remains is an abstract representation of the original interactions. On the face of it, this process of abstraction is nothing new. It is impossible to fully represent every interaction in successive conversations or texts. We live by this kind of inference (Goffman, 1959), and the capacity to generalize in this way is the source of all human communication (Zijderveld, 1970). The important contribution of the Montreal School, however, is to demonstrate that this process of abstraction through distanciation becomes a source of authority for collective action. Through distanciation, abstract representations tend to shed any trace of specific authorship. That is, the actions and intentions of particular individuals are omitted in subsequent interactions, and the resulting textual representations (abstractions) are the primary means by which we communicate with each other. It is this 'vanishing' (Taylor & Van Every, 2011) of authorship that gives abstractions their authority. As the contributions of specific individuals get lost in the distancing of texts, more and more agency is attributed to the textual abstraction itself. Consequently, the textual abstraction becomes reified – taken as given – in ways that convey power. Authority is now attributed to the textual abstraction itself rather than any particular individual.

(Koschmann, 2013, p. 68)

This phenomenon of distanciation is evident across social media platforms as content (including ideas, intentions, discourse and other textual products) can be rapidly and continuously edited or adjusted to fit the needs of the current producer/consumer, the format of the given technology (image, tweet, blog, video, audio, etc.), and the discursive effects of other texts in that network.

Given that tumultuous nature of organization within social media, the Montreal School perspective on organizing and organization is a useful one to employ. Cooren in Schoeneborn et al. (2014) describes an organization as a hybrid,

it is made of various ontologies that are organized and recognized to a greater or lesser extent. Taylor and Van Every (2000) would also say that it is an interrelated network of communication processes, a position that appears, to some extent, compatible with social systems theory.

(p. 293)

This approach fits well with Weick's own view of organization as a process of becoming, a state of organizing, which is ongoing and social in nature. At the same time, I heed Putnam and Nicotera's (2009) suggestion that we need not limit ourselves to just one perspective within CCO, as insights from the other two schools of thought offer complementary tools of analysis and may respond to gaps in the others. For example, the Four Flows approach (McPhee & Zaug, 2000) offers a useful framework for understanding processes of member negotiation within organization which works well from a CSM perspective as a flow of organizing.

Cooren et al. (2011, p. 1159) point out that CCO provides a valuable perspective on organizational identity and "connects with recent interests in organizational identity from a discourse perspective (i.e. Leclercq-Vandelannoitte, 2011)." From this perspective CCO and current work on discourse and identity continue to reflect organizations as "socially constructed from networks of conversations or dialogues" (Humphreys & Brown, 2002, p. 422). Taylor and Cooren (1997) have laid the groundwork for further understandings of organizational identity as existing only as "discourse where its reality is created, and sustained" (p. 429). Subsequent work in this vein has expanded theory on the communicatively constituted nature of organizations to address ways in which individual voices may connect to broader, organizational perspectives, thus opening a path of inquiry into the relationships between individual sensemaking around organizing and the collective organization (i.e. Taylor & Cooren, 1997, Taylor & Van Every, 2000).

Although there is a growing literature in the CCO tradition which investigates the importance of technology within the paradigm (Kavada, 2015), there has not been a great deal of work done specifically in the area of social media from within the CCO tradition. Nevertheless, there has been some interest in technology within the broader organizational communication literature from a number of different perspectives. Building on the work of theorists such as Wanda Orlikowski (1992), researchers working from the CCO approach (Kavada, 2015) have begun to investigate the importance of technology within social processes, collective sensemaking and issues of power.

Digital media may represent new channels of communication, yet they are still defined by social processes embedded in conversations, texts, interactions and sensemaking. As a result, social media communication surfaces experiences and interactions that may previously have gone unspoken or undocumented within organizations. For that reason, digital media networks offer a rich site of inquiry for CCO scholars who wish to explore the processes through which organizational identities are formed and maintained through time. To that end, social media networks themselves can be theorized as communicatively constituted sites of organizing. Koschmann (2013, p. 68), drawing upon the work of the Montreal School, conceptualizes collective identities as textual phenomenon, 'authoritative texts' that represent an "abstract textual representation of the collective that portrays its structure and direction, showing how activities are coordinated and indicating relations of authority." Similarly, Kuhn (2008) defines text as a 'network of meanings' that reflect the linguistic interactions between network members. Kuhn then explains that these texts become authoritative when they develop a 'dominant reading.'

Although we may conceptualize organizational identities as authoritative texts, constituted through communication, theorists still struggle with questions regarding agency and power within and through these texts. Social media networks may provide insights into how communicative processes impact these specific networks, and how issues of power and agency in identity construction are reflected in these platforms. Furthermore, these networks may lack a clear picture of their members. Generally speaking, an organization establishes a somewhat fixed and visible membership base (Ahrne & Brunsson, 2011) that ensures the "succession of its constitutive communication process and therefore increases the organization's chances of perpetuation" (Blaschke et al., 2012, p. 966). In her work on communication technology, Thorhauge (2012), takes a CCO perspective to investigate the use of social media as a channel of organizational communication between professors and students in a university environment. And Boyd and Ellison (2007) concur in that social media reflect very different aspects of organizational life than more traditional forms of organizational technology, concluding that social media represent a new and different way of understanding and accessing social networks.

Public relations and communication scholars also face a number of challenges when attempting to assess the dynamics of social media from both a theoretical and a practice perspective. Previous understandings of how organizing and identity are constituted in terms of communicative processes are changing within the new media environment. What may have previously been experienced as face-to-face communication between organizational members has moved into a Web-based digital format. One of the defining characteristics of social media is, however, that there exists now a durable record of this communicative interaction. The function of the network is to produce text-based communication, or in the case of YouTube or Flickr, for example, video or photographic texts. From an organizational perspective, agency in this network can be problematic as the human and non-human actants circulate through the network, text in particular moving away from its author and in to relationships with other texts, other authors and ideas that may or not reflect the mission or vision of the organization collectively.

The importance of text as a physical artifact, or 'stable' form of communication has been outlined by Cooren (2004) in his discussion of the implications of textual agency within organizations. These texts (digital in the case of social media, or physical in the sense of memos, letters, documents and contracts) participate, along with other elements of organization, to produce text which serve to define and structure the organization. Cooren points out that by 'remaining' these texts establish conversations in fixed points of time. The question of timeframe within both CCO theory and the CSM framework is interesting. Although sensemaking may be bracketed between a trigger (or shock) and the restoration of routine, the process itself is retrospective. Likewise, social media technologies are very difficult to pin down in terms of locating a particular idea at a point in time. The question of temporal location within organizing is one that continues to challenge scholars in both CSM and CCO. Nevertheless, how or whenever, the texts emerge, they also document sensemaking processes, identifying contributions to the textual conversation unfolding. These documents are also disseminated beyond just those individuals engaged in the interaction, but made available to any member of the network and possibly beyond.

There is little doubt that social media networks may offer effective communicative processes to enable organizing around the constitution of shared identity (Kahn & Kellner, 2004). However, participation in identity construction online can also present challenges to authenticity. As a recent perspective on social media for change suggests,

> Facebook, in particular, can increase participation in social movements – if you call a single click of the mouse participation. More than a million people have joined a Facebook page of the Save Darfur Coalition, but few among them have taken any additional action to help those in Sudan.
>
> (Wilson Quarterly, 2011)

From a CCO perspective, networks as sites of organizing represent the social media experience as more than just a change of context in terms of communication and relationships. It may ultimately be an extension of self in that, as Turkle (1995) asserts, these media are not just changing our lives, the way we work and communicate – but they are profoundly changing ourselves, our identities and challenging our authenticity. Turkle's Alone Together suggests that technologically mediated communication, like that conducted through social media networks, separates people from the processing of their emotions, and presents confusing identities (Turkle, 2011). This tension between identity construction as an individual, and collective identity construction through a process of organizing, is highlighted in the social media environment. As organizational membership is negotiated, questions of who we are and how things are done here reflect rapid changes in both the organization and the agency surrounding both human and nonhuman elements in that network.

The CCO perspective can provide valuable insights into processes of identity construction within this digital context; however, CCO theory alone does not give us the complete picture. Bisel (2010, p. 129) points to the need to expand the work of CCO theory further, so as to acknowledge that communication is a necessary condition for the constitution of organizing, "but it is not sufficient to ensure organizing will be called into being." This call for further work leads us to reflect again on the question posed in Chapter 1, why do some organizational identities persist and become durable, and others do not? What is the communicative condition under which organizations move into becoming, and identities emerge as plausible to prospective or newly enrolled organizational members? In order to unpack this question further, I will discuss the potential of the CSM (Critical Sense-making) framework as a compatible and complementary frame of analysis through which to investigate the multi-faceted relationships between organizing and communication in the following chapter. By drawing connections between these two frameworks, I will set the foundation for further investigation of processes of social media organizing as illustrated in the case studies to follow.

3 Critical Sensemaking (CSM) in a virtual environment

In this chapter, I provide a detailed discussion of the CSM framework (Helms Mills, Thurlow & Mills, 2010; Helms Mills, 2003), expanding upon the micro-level psycho-social properties of sensemaking and making connections to the critical context in which these properties operate. This will provide the necessary tools to evaluate how virtual identities are made meaningful through social media as future chapters present examples of identity enacted. CSM offers a useful method of understanding power and its influence on processes of organizing and identity construction. Drawing on the sensemaking property of plausibility in particular, I investigate how some organizational identities are made meaningful, as both plausible and legitimate, among organizational members and audiences.

The previous chapter reviewed the CCO perspective and provided a theoretical foundation for the analysis to follow. However, although the CCO perspective offers important insights into the communicative constitution of identity, it is somewhat limited in its focus on agency. Consistent with Townley's (1994, p. 107) caution that "it would be a mistake to assume that the individual is a passive participant in the constitution of identity," this investigation of identity within a social media context is concerned with the role of agency in the production and maintenance of those identities.

From the CCO perspective, McPhee and Zaug (2009) argued that "all communication has constitutive force" in that all communication "constitutes socially recognized agency" and calls relationships into being (p. 28). In addition, McPhee and Zaug assert that "although communication relatively straightforwardly constitutes the agency of the communicating parties and aspects of their relationship, the constitution of outside objects, especially complex organizations, is itself more complex" (p. 28). In this chapter, I present the CSM framework as a way of understanding the process of sensemaking between individuals and organizations, with connections to the 'outside objects' or the broader societal context in which communication occurs.

The origins of both CCO theory and CSM are intertwined with the work of Karl Weick (1969, 1979, 1995) in that they both start from the perspective of organizations as social constructions produced through forms of communication. Weick (1969) advocated for an understanding of organization as an action, organizing. His view of organizations saw them as produced (often communicatively) action by action, in a constant state of becoming. This process-oriented view of ongoing sensemaking is a useful one for understanding organizational identity within the impermanent and precarious processes of social media networks. At the same time, sensemaking offers a useful framework for analyzing language relationships. Language, as seen through this framework, is the substance of sensemaking. "Sense is generated by words that are combined into the sentences of conversation to convey something about our ongoing experience" (Weick, 1995, p. 106). But the process is ongoing as individuals pull their understandings from a variety of vocabularies; occupational, professional, social, ideological. And, there is always some "slippage" between the meanings conveyed and understood (Weick, 1995, p. 107).

Weick's view of sensemaking is predicated on the assumption that individuals (on their own and collectively) prefer stability in their interactions with meaning and identity. That is to say, we prefer to sort out or settle upon a meaning associated with a particular identity, event, language, or process and then our sensemaking around that is relatively stable and easier to navigate. In the course of making sense of identities Weick (1995) suggests that these routines become established and "encourage and stabilize certain forms of sensemaking" (Helms Mills, 2003, p. 54).

Within the more recent organizational studies literature, the term sensemaking is used in a variety of different ways. This definition from Klein, Moon, and Hoffman (2006) offers a good description of how sensemaking is understood in this volume, and how I will use this idea in conjunction with the CCO perspectives we have discussed thus far:

> By sensemaking, modern researchers seem to mean something different from creativity, comprehension, curiosity, mental modeling, explanation, or situational awareness, although all these factors or phenomena can be involved in or related to sensemaking. Sensemaking is a motivated, continuous effort to understand connections (which can be among people, places, and events) in order to anticipate their trajectories and act effectively.
>
> (p. 71)

This connection between understanding and action is key to the sensemaking process. Weick (1995) proposes that, in essence, changes in organizational sensemaking must be triggered – separately from the day to day sensemaking that stabilizes organizational life. At that point, through sensemaking, "people must enact order into chaos" (Weick et al., 2005, p. 411)

Weick further explains the sensemaking, although ongoing, is still a process with a starting point. These punctuated points in an ongoing exercise are referred to as shocks or junctures, and they essentially act as triggers. Helms Mills (2003) describes these shocks as occasions of ambiguity or uncertainty that create breaks in organizational routines. These might include organizational mergers, changes in work routines, organizational crises, etc.

It is important to note, however, that sensemaking goes beyond interpretation. It is more than simply trying to figure out what is going on. As Maitlis and Christianson (2014, p. 58) explain, "sensemaking involves the active authoring of events and frameworks for understanding, as people play a role in constructing the very situations they attempt to comprehend (Sutcliffe, 2013; Weick, 1995; Weick et al., 2005)."

Starting from a shock in the routine of day to day communicative and organizational process, our own sensemaking begins with Weick's (1979) seven properties of sensemaking within organizations. These psycho-social properties allow us to see processes which organizational members engage with as they construct meaning about the world around them. These properties identify for us that sensemaking is: (1) grounded in identity construction, (2) retrospective, (3) enactive of sensible environments, (4) social, (5) ongoing, (6) focused on and by extracted cues and (7) driven by plausibility rather than accuracy.

Grounded in identity construction: Identity construction is an essential component of sensemaking not just as it relates to individual and organizational identities, but because it "influences how other aspects, or properties of the sensemaking process are understood" (Helms Mills, 2003, p. 55). At the same time, the process of identity construction itself is influenced by what others think. This is arguably the foundational property at work in all of our sensemaking activities. This property suggests that our identity is continually being redefined as a result of experiences and contact with others. This includes previous experiences, both within the organization and beyond, from our past work experience, our childhood, friends, education, family or other influential factors. Although identity can change over time, ultimately individuals strive to find sensemaking alternatives which support their own interpretation of their identities as organizational members.

Gioia and Thomas (1996) suggest that managers can change the image of the organization that they send to outsiders. And if the outsiders respond by accepting that image, and reply with meaning that reinforces the new image, then organizational reflection may occur as a catalyst for identity change. This shift to an understanding of identity as fluid and collectively constructed has opened the door to a range of scholarship investigating the processes at work, both individual and collective, in the constitution of identity. Identity construction as a sensemaking property is seen as an ongoing process where "people learn about their identities by projecting them into an environment and observing the consequences." Consequently, Weick's (1995, p. 23) sensemaking has emerged as a lens through which investigation into the ways in which individuals construct their identities can be made. Furthermore, it provides an opportunity to investigate the process by which changes to identity become plausible, or are made meaningful. This perspective has clear implications when considering identity construction in socially networked environments.

Retrospective: Weick (1979) explains through this property that we rely on past experiences to interpret current events. Thus, sensemaking is a comparative process, whereby we relate the present situation to our knowledge of the past. As a result, we cannot know what we make of a situation or experience until we reflect upon our previous experiences which inform our present.

In his 1988 work on sensemaking in crisis situations, Weick draws on an example from Bateson (1972) to illustrate this point. He starts with the example, "an explorer can never know what he is exploring until it has been explored" (Bateson, 1972, p. xvi). He then further explains how the retrospective nature of sensemaking comes into play.

> Bateson's description of exploring illustrates the key point about sensemaking the explorer cannot know what he is facing until he faces it, and then looks back over the episode to sort out what happened, a sequence that involves retrospective sensemaking. But the act of exploring itself has an impact on what is being explored, which means that parts of what the explorer discovers retrospectively are consequences of his own making. Furthermore, the exploring itself is guided by preconceptions of some kind, even though they may be generic preconceptions such as 'this will have made sense once I explore it although right now it seems senseless'(Weick, Gilfillan, & Keith, 1973).
>
> (Weick, 1988, p. 306)

As Weber and Glynn (2006, p. 1647) point out, Weick maintained that "sensemaking never starts. The reason it never starts is that pure duration never stops. People are always in the middle of things, which become things, only when those people focus on the past from some point of view" (Weick, 1995, p. 43). Creating meaning is thus retrospective in nature, an "attentional process . . . to that which has already occurred" (Weick, 1995, p. 25).

Focused on and by Extracted Cues: Cues also shape sensemaking as it unfolds, since sensemaking is "focused on and by extracted cues" (Weick, 1995, p. 49), in a process in which individuals "interpret and explain set of cues from their environments" (Maitlis, 2005, p. 21).

Weick suggests that our communicative environments are too cluttered or full of potential cues. Therefore, we must choose to attend to some cues while completely ignoring others. As we piece together those cues, we begin to make sense of things. Since sensemaking is retrospective, past experiences, including rules and regulations, dictate what cues we will extract to make sense of a situation. In the modern communication environment, individuals are overwhelmed with messages, images and text. It is impossible to take in all the communicative cues of a modern, socially mediated digital environment. Therefore, individuals must extract certain cues which appear relevant or plausible to their current sensemaking.

Driven by Plausibility Rather than Accuracy: This sensemaking property highlights the point that we do not rely on the accuracy of our perceptions during sensemaking. Actually, we search to identify cues that make our sensemaking seem plausible. In doing so, we may distort or eliminate what is accurate in favor of what appears to be a plausible meaning. Plausibility is a sensemaking property that may be visible in conjunction with the others, as it underpins which cues we extract from a network, or what identity resonates with our experience of an organization.

To deal with ambiguity, interdependent people search for meaning, settle for plausibility, and move on. These are moments of sensemaking, and scholars stretch those moments, scrutinize them and name them in the belief that they affect how action gets routinized, flux gets tamed, objects get enacted, and precedents get set (Weick et al., 2005, p. 419).

Mills and Weatherbee (2006, p. 270) point out in their study on sensemaking as a framework to understand disasters, that Weick has indicated the properties of identity construction and plausibility are more central than other properties to the sensemaking process (Weick et al., 2005, p. 416). They agree with that assessment, and add "that identity construction is at the root of sensemaking as it influences how other aspects, or properties of the sensemaking process are understood" (Helms Mills, 2003, p. 55). Plausibility works with identity construction, and other properties, to restore order to a chaotic environment. Thus, we believe that identity construction is about "who we think we are [and it] shapes how we enact and how we interpret" (Weick et al., 2005, p. 416). This makes it pivotal to the sensemaking process and helps to determine what is understood as plausible or not.

Enactive of the Environment: This property suggests that sensemaking is about making sense of an experience within our environment. Thus, our sensemaking can be either constrained or enhanced by the very environment that it has created. Similar to a self-fulfilling prophecy, this property maintains that the identity that has been created by the sensemaker reinforces their own sense of legitimacy.

Maitlis and Christianson (2014, p. 67) explain that

> A critical fourth feature of sensemaking concerns the action that people take to make sense of a situation which, in turn, enacts the environment that they seek to understand. Thus, it has been argued that sensemaking creates 'rational accounts of the world that enable action' (Maitlis, 2005, p. 21), is 'a continuous effort to understand connections (which can be among people, places, and events) in order to anticipate their trajectories and act effectively' (Klein et al., 2006), and is 'enactive of sensible environments' (Weick, 1995, p. 30). These action-meaning cycles occur repeatedly as people construct provisional understandings that they continuously enact and modify. We thus define sensemaking as:

a process, prompted by violated expectations, that involves attending to and bracketing cues in the environment, creating intersubjective meaning through cycles of interpretation and action, and thereby enacting a more ordered environment from which further cues can be drawn."

Social: Sensemaking is a process that cannot happen in isolation. It is dependent upon our interactions with others, whether they are actually present at the site of sensemaking or not. In addition, we will be influenced by social structures such as an organization's rules, routines, symbols and language as these provide scripts for appropriate conduct. But when routines or scripts do not exist, an individual must fall back on past experience and his or her own sensemaking.

This property is described very well by Maitlis and Christianson (2014, p. 66) as follows:

> In contrast, other definitions position sensemaking as a social process that occurs between people, as meaning is negotiated, contested, and mutually co- constructed. 'Social' is one of Weick's (1995) seven key properties of sense- making. Weick et al. (2005, p. 409) elaborate that sensemaking unfolds 'in a social context of other actors' and Maitlis (2005, p. 21) describes organizational sensemaking as 'a fundamentally social process' in which 'organization members interpret their environment in and through interactions with each other, constructing accounts that allow them to comprehend the world and act collectively.' This stance sees sensemaking as the 'discursive processes of constructing and interpreting the social world' (Gephart, 1993, p. 1485).

Ongoing: Sensemaking is a process that never stops. Weick suggests that we are constantly making sense of our environments. And although this process is ongoing, there are moments or shocks where our established routines and understandings of the environment are challenged. Weick maintains that we isolate those moments and cues from this continuous sensemaking to make sense of the current situation, which we will be 'forced' to attend to, because of the disruption in our routine.

The potential of these properties as analytic tools is debated in the literature, and the sensemaking framework itself is unclear in its presentation as to whether it is a framework, a method, a theory or a lens on the organizational world. Originally referred to as "a set of explanatory ideas" Weick (1995, p. xi) has also defined sensemaking as a recipe that provides both a way to interpret the environment and a guide to action. A recipe can help to make retrospective sense out of observed behavior, or in a more active sense, a recipe "tells how to handle people and situations so that satisfactory results are obtained and so that undesirable consequences are minimized" (Weick, 1979, p. 46). However, sensemaking can perhaps most usefully be understood as an heuristic for gaining insights into how individuals connect with stories of organizational identity on a micro-level, as they construct the day-to-day activities of organizations.

In his earlier work, Weick presented these seven interrelated properties as all equally important to the sensemaking process, although one or another could be more dominant depending on the sensemaking event. More recent work has acknowledged that these properties appear to weight differently in the process (Weick et al., 2005). For example, in an effort to ensure a plausible meaning is constructed, individuals may selectively extract cues or seek endorsement from a specific social network with a similar understanding of the situation. As well, the seven properties of sensemaking referred to earlier are not all equally visible in the process of individual sensemaking in terms of analysis. At times one or more of the properties may play a more significant role in influencing sensemaking than others. In addition to this, the sensemaking properties may influence individual sensemaking simultaneously. For example, the property of enactment may become visible in a particular sensemaking process, but that same enactment of meaning may influence the plausibility of other actions, and simultaneously the construction of individual identity. As individuals enact their beliefs, they also make sense of them. And in effect, the use of language in the describing of an event enacts the construction of sensemaking about the event. As a result, individuals within organizations may not make sense of the same event in the same way. To that end, there is no one 'right' meaning attached to a given experience.

Within the sensemaking literature there is considerable debate around how these seven properties facilitate or enact sensemaking processes. In Weick's early work he was somewhat, and perhaps purposely, vague on the ways in which sensemaking is accomplished and how individuals and agency factor into that process. Likewise, applications of sensemaking as a methodological framework have been fragmented in their approach, some focusing on sensemaking as an individual process (i.e. Klein, Moon, & Hoffman, 2006) while others focus on the process as a shared and collective approach (i.e. Maitlis, 2005). In the Maitlis and Christianson (2014) review of the organizational sensemaking literature, the authors identify two central areas of debate within the literature, namely "where sensemaking takes place and when sensemaking occurs – which reflect fundamentally different assumptions about the nature of sensemaking" (p. 94).

These reflect the ontological perspectives of sensemaking, getting at the nature of sensemaking itself. The first question, where sensemaking takes place, refers to the debate around whether or not sensemaking is an individual or a collective process. As Maitlis and Christianson (2014) describe it, "scholars locate sensemaking in different places: some regard it as a primarily cognitive process that takes place largely in individuals' heads, and others see it as process of social construction that is carried out through interaction between people" (p. 94). More recent work from a CSM perspective comes from a starting point of sensemaking as a social constructivist endeavor, and working in conjunction with the CCO theoretical framework, this approach makes sense for our study of social media.

The second point of debate within the literature regards the temporal direction of sensemaking. For the most part, Weickian sensemaking and the CSM tradition that emerges from it takes an historical or at least retrospective perspective, i.e. we can't make sense of something until we experience it. However, some more recent work has proposed a future-oriented or prospective approach (i.e. Wiebe, 2010). As Maitlis and Christianson (2014) summarize,

> Gephart et al. (2010) propose that future-oriented sensemaking (constructing meanings that create images of the future) is embedded in past and present temporal states and uses past and present temporal orientations to provide contexts for proposed future entities. Consistent with these ideas of embedded temporalities, Stigliani and Ravasi (2012), in their study of design teams, theorize that prospective sensemaking is based on interrelated cycles of retrospection. Wiebe (2010) argues more generally for a broader temporal basis to sensemaking. His examination of 'temporal sensemaking' in organizational change found that people make sense of the timing and pace of their experiences, constructing the 'same' mandated change through very different temporal lenses. This led to accounts of the change that ranged from 'no change' to 'massive and unrelenting change' (Wiebe, 2010). He concludes that a conception of sensemaking as retrospective ignores the present, which is where sensemaking takes place, but that engaging in sensemaking in the present involves drawing on all three dimensions of temporality.
>
> (p. 97)

There is general agreement among researchers that sensemaking must be triggered or prompted, but from that point onward the importance and function of the psycho-social properties is a source of debate. Likewise, the ways in which properties such as identity and plausibility may work to privilege some meanings over others is not addressed through sensemaking alone.

Critiques of Weickian sensemaking note that the framework of seven properties itself suggests a scientific or positivist approach proposing that there are methodologically distinguishable cognitive processes which influence how people think or feel about an event. This scientific approach to sensemaking does not take into account the rhetorical and discursive influences operating within this framework, nor the social interactions of individuals engaged in the process. Further critique points out that Weick's framework fails to address power within this process. Helms Mills and Mills (2000) advocate for a more nuanced treatment of power within sensemaking, highlighting that the discursive effects of power serve to ultimately limit the range of possible meanings from which individuals may make sense of a given event.

From the discursive approach to sensemaking, there is a substantive and growing body of literature which tackles research on narratives and storytelling (Maitlis et al., 2014). I am particularly interested in this work from a social media perspective, as the very essence of socially networked digital communication is the production and dissemination of narratives across platforms and among audiences. In this way, collective sensemaking can evolve very rapidly and across distances which were previously inaccessible. The importance of narrative in this process highlights the essential nature of narrative construction to human sensemaking broadly speaking. As Polkinghorne (1998, p. 1) asserts, narrative is "the primary form by which human experience is made meaningful."

Sensemaking scholars have addressed forms and applications of narrative storytelling in a variety of ways over the past two decades. As Maitlis and Christianson (2014). point out:

> A great benefit of examining organizational sensemaking through a narrative lens is that it reveals not only who is involved and what they are doing but also the meanings that they are constructing in the process. As such, it spotlights the plurivocality of organizations and the much contested nature of organizational meanings. It does so by uncovering the very different stories told by different groups and showing how even a dominant organizational narrative can be embellished and modified by less powerful individuals in ways that significantly change its meaning.
>
> (p. 81)

A number of scholars have addressed narrative in sensemaking over the past two decades (for example, (Brown, Stacey, & Nandhakumar, 2008; Currie & Brown, 2003; Humphreys & Brown, 2002, who have investigated the contested nature of identity construction as organizational members vie to surface preferred narratives as dominant within the sensemaking process. Likewise, Boje (1991) and Rhodes (2001) have added their work to the growing body of research on the plurality and polyphonic nature of narratives emerging from processes of organizing. As Maitlis and Christianson (2014) suggest, this process of negotiating space for organizational narratives can reflect tensions within the organization as "Sensemaking is the process through which these narratives are contested and collective accounts negotiated." They add that "since narratives serve to support different parties' identity and legitimacy claims, agreement, if reached, is often temporary and produces fragile shared accounts (Brown et al., 2008; Patriotta, 2003)" (p. 81).

According to Weick, we make sense by seeing a world on which we have already imposed what we believe. Our previous sensemaking has shaped the boundaries through which we see plausible meanings. Helms Mills

(2003) applies a critical perspective to this process by suggesting that power relationships may privilege the views of more powerful actors A number of studies using a CSM approach have looked specifically at the power of individual actors whose sensemaking has been privileged over that of others in the organization. For example, Hartt et al. (2014) combines a CSM approach with an Actor Network Theory (ANT) theoretical framework to unravel the complex sensemaking processes involving powerful actors operating within the Air Canada organization and its environment. And in the context of a Space Agency, Ruel (2018) looks at the lack of gender balance among actors in this organization and the subsequent impact on gendered sensemaking.

Within the CSM framework, one tool that has been used to tease out the importance of individual actors is the application of organizational rules (Mills & Murgatroyd, 1991) to sensemaking processes. Organizational rules suggest that the relationships that privilege certain identities above others may be identified through observation of the 'ways we do things' or the rules, formal and informal, which govern how organizations work. Helms-Mills points out, however, that organizational rules alone cannot explain how rules are interpreted and enacted (2003, p. 196).

To address some of these gaps in the sensemaking framework, and to specifically engage in a discussion of power within organizations and in the construction of organizational identities, I turn to Critical Sensemaking (Helms Mills, Thurlow, & Mills, 2010) for a more robust approach. CSM extends and expands the context in which the sensemaking process occurs. This context includes issues of power and privilege in the process of understanding why some language, social practices and experiences become meaningful for individuals and others do not (Thurlow, 2010). Individuals do not make sense of their experiences in isolation of their broader environments. Individual actors within the same organization may have more influence on meaning than others. Individuals with more power in organizations may also exert more power on the sensemaking of other organizational members as they extract cues or enact meanings. Critical sensemaking provides a lens through which to analyze the power relationships reflected in these inequalities and the consequences of those power effects for individuals.

Starting with the sensemaking properties at the micro, individual level, CSM then provides perspective at the organizational level with the introduction of organizational rules. From there, the CSM approach expands the lens further by addressing the formative context in which the organization exists. Formative contexts (Blackler, 1992) are structures that serve to constrain or define what meanings are plausible within the societal-level context of the organization. Within the CSM framework, formative contexts serve as a bridge between dominant social values and individual action. While no one formative context is necessary or fixed, some are privileged within society above others. As a result, these contexts are experienced as a restrictive influence on organizational rules and individual enactment of meaning through the privileging of certain dominant social values or assumptions. Formative contexts, and the related organizational rules, are both productive of, and produced through discourse. By introducing the dimension of formative contexts, the critical sensemaking framework creates space for a discussion of how the macro-level context in which organizations and individuals operate impacts the range of possibilities available for sensemaking in terms of cues that may be extracted, the plausibility of various text and narratives, and the nature of enactment (Helms Mills et al., 2010).

The CMS approach offers important insight into why some meanings are acted upon as organizational identities are constituted, while others are not. Miller (2004, p. 212) explains that "sensemaking is both an individual psychological process (belief-driven by recipes) and an interactive social process (action-driven through communication cycles)." This dual process of understanding and communicating is central to the micro-level enactment of, and therefore the production, maintenance and constraint of, macro-level discourse. Sensemaking alone does not explain how some sensemaking events are developed in the first instance (whose interests are being served, what does power look like in this situation) and it does not explain how decisions are constrained by contexts and rules and how there can be an unequal distribution of power within those contexts.

Although the sensemaking properties provide a useful lens through which to analyze agency, Helms Mills (2003) reminds us that individuals do not determine their own sensemaking separate from external forces, macro-level discourse and power. By introducing the dimension of formative contexts, the critical sensemaking framework creates space for a discussion of how the macro-level context in which individuals operate affects the cues they extract, the plausibility of various text and narratives, and the nature of enactment. Mills and Murgatroyd (1991) indicate that organizational rules may also contribute to the establishment of the context in which sensemaking happens. "Rules are phenomena whose basic characteristic is that of generally controlling, constraining, guiding and defining social action" (Mills & Murgatroyd, 1991, p. 3). As such, rules provide a pre-existing sensemaking tool that contributes to the plausibility of an interpretation or the likelihood of a cue to be extracted as meaningful. The incorporation of organizational rules into the critical sensemaking framework also introduces the concept of meta rules to sensemaking practices. These rules (including privatization, competition and modes of production) are broad in scope and represent points of intersection between a number of formative contexts (Helms Mills, 2003).

In as much as rules inform our understanding of how organizations may retain unity and cohesiveness, they "simultaneously serve to contain differences of opinion, beliefs, and values while resulting in practices that give the appearance of unity of purpose" (Helms Mills & Mills, 2000a, p. 58). This perspective within a framework of critical sensemaking provides insight into both the power of the actors enacting rules, and the constraints under which these rules are introduced to the organizations. Although powerful actors in the organization may set the direction for the rules which will provide a sense of cohesion within the organization, they are themselves constrained by meta-rules and formative contexts which limit the availability of the alternatives which may be selected from within a broader discourse of organizational change.

Rules theory (Mills & Murgatroyd, 1991) offers an explanation for the consequences interpretation has on the behavior and enactment of sensemaking, and subsequently the culture of the organization. These rules also provide insight into the system of both formal and informal rules which inform organizational processes and controls. Rules combine within organizations to define the particular way things are done. The evolution of these rules may come through the effects of organizational discourse, and the subsequent experiences and behaviors of individuals within the organization. As in the construction of all knowledge/power relationships, these rules in local context are not static and may change based on the actions of individuals who resist them (Mills & Murgatroyd, 1991).

In the social media realm this tension between rules and sensemaking is perhaps even more visible as individual organizational members produce content within the social media texts that alternatively reflect, produce or challenge their own identities. Power in these networks is complicated. The tangible elements of numbers of friends, or numbers of re-tweets, do not necessarily reflect the discursive effects of the meanings being constructed. The social networks are constantly evolving, their memberships are relatively fluid, the format of communication is determined or constrained by the format of the medium, and meanings, and therefore identities are constantly being negotiated.

At the macro level, the formative context also provides a framework for the societal level discourses in which these rules operate. Helms Mills (2003) draws on Unger to provide insight into the discursive power of macro-level language and ideas. Other work in CSM has used a Foucauldian approach to power (Thurlow, 2007; Leclercq-Vandelannoitte, 2011). In these studies Foucault's description of power as relational and fluid underpins the ongoing and changing nature of the context in which meaning is constructed. The power/knowledge relationship in these examples informs the way that some meanings are privileged over others in a given sensemaking process.

When analyzed from the perspective of critical sensemaking, two properties – identity construction and plausibility – play a significant role in the link between 'concepts' as macro-level discourse and individual sensemaking. Individual identity as discussed in Weick's sensemaking process is also central to the concept of organizational identity construction. As organizations strive to build, change or maintain their corporate identities, they are essentially attempting to provide a way of conceptualizing 'who we are' as an organization. Arguably, identities result from prior beliefs and experiences, ongoing interactions and the retrospective process of sensemaking that individuals use to reconcile their social, organizational identities. Thus, new identities take form and exist as they are put into language by individuals and organizations.

By highlighting the importance of identity in the relationship between language and power in organizations, critical sensemaking offers a method of analysis which privileges the role of the individual. For example, although everyone in the organization may take part in sensemaking, there is an inherent inequality among organizational members that may affect the realities they construct (Helms Mills & Mills, 2000, p. 67). Critical sensemaking provides a lens through which to analyze the power relationships reflected in these inequalities and the consequences of those power effects for individuals. As Helms Mills (2003, p. 55) points out, identity construction "is at the root of sensemaking, and influences how other aspects or properties of the sensemaking process are understood." From that perspective, the identities of organizational members influence the way in which they make sense of events and enact meanings. This facilitates a process of identity construction where, "who we think we are (identity) as organizational actors shapes what we enact and how we interpret, which affects what outsiders think we are (image)and how they treat us, which stabilizes or destabilizes our identity" (Weick et al., 2005, p. 416).

The importance of this relationship between identity and sensemaking is significant in the enactment of meaning. As Weick et al. (2005, p. 416) reminds us, "when people face an unsettling difference, that difference often translates into questions such as who are we, what are we doing, what matters, and why does it matter? These are not trivial questions."

Along with identity construction, plausibility is the other property that provides significant influence on sensemaking to privilege some meanings, or identities, over others. Within sensemaking Weick tells us that plausibility refers to a sense of the way in which one meaning or explanation resonates more than another. It is a feeling that contained in the range of possible explanations available to sensemakers in a given situation, one feels more 'right' than the others. There is no specific definition of what makes a particular explanation plausible; however, Weick (1979) suggests that options make most sense when there are no better alternatives, other individuals seem enthusiastic about this alternative, other individuals or organizations have taken this same perspective, and/or this explanation resonates most closely with existing identities and perceptions. The CSM perspective further suggests that plausibility is also enhanced by those same factors that privilege some discourses above others. The discursive power of the actor proposing a particular manner in which to make sense of an experience, the access individuals have to a plurality of discourse, and in fact, the access individuals have to the proposed meaning, all influence plausibility. Plausibility helps to explain why we privilege some things over others and how we might have different interpretations of the same event. In terms of critical sensemaking, plausibility is linked to legitimacy and power because of the weight it gives to the sensemaking of some over others.

In the following chapter I will describe the methodology that is applied throughout the examples of identity construction within socially mediated environments which follow. This methodology will combine both CCO theory and the CSM framework described here to develop a deeper understanding of the process of organizational identity construction within social media networks.

4 Methodology

This chapter explains the methodological approach used to investigate the case studies of organizational identity in the following chapters. As discussed in the previous chapters, useful synergies exist between the conceptual frameworks of CCO and CSM. Although each of these approaches offers paths of analysis for text and context in identity construction, neither alone has offered a comprehensive and established method of empirical analysis. In the following chapters, I will analyze several examples of organizations involved in identity construction and engaged with social media. For each of these cases I have employed strategies and tools of both CCO and CSM in order to identify both the micro-level processes at work among organizational members, audiences and the macro-level social media networks through which they interact. Most importantly, this method allows for the study of organizational identity construction as an ongoing and emergent process within a broader network of conversation.

To gather the empirical material for this research I employed a variety of web-based tools. Initially, I applied a specific social media network analyzer called Netlytic. This is a "cloud-based text and social networks analyzer that can automatically summarize large volumes of text and discover social networks from conversations on social media sites such as Twitter, Facebook, Instagram, YouTube, blogs, online forums and chats" (https://netlytic.org/). It is very sophisticated in its approach, as it allows researchers to build and visualize communication networks to discover and explore emerging social connections between individuals within online communities, and to see a flow of communication, indicated in the shape of the visual representation, providing insights into the nature of the two-way relationships. I gained useful insights into the network maps and relationships through this material. However, it became clear throughout the analysis of data that other tools and approaches would also have to be incorporated in order to gain a more complete picture of the context in which the organizations, and their networks, exist. To that end, the analytic process identified in this research includes Netlytic data analysis combined with other network analysis tools such as Google analytics, Hootsuite and Klout. As a result, a more multi-dimensional analytic process has emerged.

It is important to note that these tools were not, in and of themselves, employed to evaluate or 'measure' social media effects which is actually the objective for which they are designed. In this research I used these tools to scrape data across a broad network of social media activity related to some specific organizational shocks which triggered sensemaking.

As previously discussed, Weick (1995) proposes that, in essence, changes in organizational sensemaking must be triggered – separately from the day to day sensemaking that stabilizes organizational life. These times of ambiguity or uncertainty create breaks in organizational routines and cause individuals and organizations to question and reflect upon their identities, before, during and after the event. Therefore, as a starting point for analysis, I looked at events in organizational sensemaking and identified an organizational crisis, an organizing of activism and the emergence of an alternative form of capitalist organizing as examples of shocks, in the routines of stabilized organizational identity.

Focusing on these events, I proceeded to gather social media text relevant to the organizations concerned, for the empirical narratives which emerged around these cases through identifiers such as hashtags, handles and organizational pages and posts. This process produces much more than just static text found in a tweet or a post. Those particular items reflect, of course, important representations of the text enacted in the conversations, but they exist within an interactive and ongoing conversation between individuals, both within and outside of organizations. The web-based tools allowed me to gather textual data as well as information on the direction and flow of communication, essentially who is speaking with whom. They allowed me to visually assess the reach of ideas and conversations across a network of individual stakeholders of the organization. They also allowed me to focus on two important aspects of the networked conceptualization of communication identified through CCO and CSM. These two aspects are referred to as nodes, which represent the individuals and organizations or groups within the social media network, and edges, which indicate the ways in which these nodes are interacting with each other, or their connections. Essentially, these two aspects visually draw a map of the network in terms of the direction and flow of information between the key elements in the communication process within a specifically limited timeframe around a specifically limited communicative event (i.e. a hashtag or organizational handle). Unraveling the connections between these points on the map offers a great deal of insight into the context surrounding the organizational communication, as well as the actual textual artifacts produced within these interactions. These processes of data gathering from within networked communication surfaced the narratives of organizational identity which revealed themselves as dominant, or at least plausible, within the network.

One of the methodological challenges of dealing with material produced in and productive of social media environments is finding a way to acknowledge and capture the context in which the text is produced. Khosravinik and Unger (2015) in their work on critical discourse analysis and social media advocate for the use of case study methodology in dealing with this issue. They advise that, "The non-linear context of communication on the participatory web indicates the usefulness of more observational research approaches, i.e. attending to communicative events rather than communicative data themselves" (p. 215). Consistent with their call for this approach, I have developed a case study context around the material gathered from the social media networks in this research. I have also employed their three broad orientations to working with text in a social media context:

1   As discourse analysts, we consider the social context of the users and their communication.
2   As critical discourse analysts, we are not satisfied with the mere description of genre, content and communication.
3   As social media scholars, we view the participatory web as part of a media apparatus that is used by individuals in society, hence we do not treat digitally mediated texts as part of a 'virtual' world that is separate from the physical world and 'reality', despite acknowledging that digitally mediated contexts have specific features that may affect our analyses (p. 216).

Using both the CCO approach, as well as the multi-faceted lens of CSM, I use a layered analysis to address these issues. In the application of the critical sensemaking framework to this analysis, the focus on text and context provided insight into the formative context and organizational rules which inform individual sensemaking. This connection from the macro to the micro ensures that the context in which the text is produced is acknowledged. To further enhance that relationship, in the application of the CCO perspective, the focus on text and context provided insight into the enactment of communication, through exchange and relationships. As Francois Cooren points out from the Montreal School perspective, "communication is, first and foremost, considered an action" (Schoeneborn et al., 2014, p. 289). He adds that communication is seen within the context of an exchange or a transaction, and that the context in which these transactions occur may include more than just humans, but also situations, realities, facts and other elements of the broader context (Schoeneborn et al., 2014).

I first look at the actions and transactions enacted through communication in the networked environment, both inside and outside the organization. To that end, this analysis defines the organizational boundaries very loosely, as the organizational identity resides, from both a CCO and a CSM perspective, both in the hands of organizational members and others external to the organization itself. Understanding communication as an exchange is consistent in many aspects with the ongoing and social nature of sensemaking. It also reflects key elements of another sensemaking property, the enacted environment. Situations, facts, realities, etc., are punctuated and made durable through actions which are productive of and produced by the social media network. For example, the re-tweeting of a message from another source. Through the analysis of the broader networked communication around particular events and organizations, the research presented in the following chapters will address empirical material from both within and outside of the organization, from the basis of plausibility and 'fact' and with a view always of the networked relationships in which the text was produced.

This is also consistent with the conceptualization of social media presented in this book as more than a repository of text-based statements, but as a transactionally oriented exchange of meanings, informed by a series of psycho-social properties, constrained and shaped within a broader formative context, and ultimately, productive of identities which are both fluid and enacted over time. By adopting an approach of critical sensemaking, this research attempts to address the dynamic of organizational identity construction in a more complete fashion as the analysis of language becomes focused on processes rather than on discrete categories of individual understanding, reflected in language. The retrospective and ongoing nature of sensemaking, and the tendency of individuals to draw on a plurality of available discourses and identities as they make sense of things, makes for an ideal framework through which to view change as a process.

Another key principle of the sensemaking process in this analysis is its focus on extracted cues. This property provides an important reference point for analysis of text from and through the social networks. Although the CCO perspective can shed some light onto the power/knowledge relationships that may maintain organizational identities, it does not completely answer for us why some identities are adopted and maintained by organizations and others are not. Cues tie elements together cognitively in a sensemaking process, and they are linked to a broader system of understanding about what is important. As individuals, or organizations, pick up on some cues, as opposed to others, they achieve relative importance in a sensemaking process (Helms Mills, 2003).

The sensemaking process is also enactive. As individuals enact their beliefs, they also make sense of them. And in effect, the use of language in the describing of an event enacts the construction of sensemaking about the event. Helms Mills (2003, p. 198) explains enactment as a property of sensemaking which "means that we create an activity that reflects our making sense of the experience within our environment." Critical sensemaking draws on organizational rules theory (Mills & Murgatroyd, 1991) to offer an analysis of how these actions are determined. In this analysis, organizational rules are identified as "activities of socialization, whereby employees enact organizational rules and maintain organizational culture" (Helms Mills, 2003, p. 199). However, the rules also set limitations on individual sensemaking and actions. This connection between the social construction of beliefs and their creation of, or constraint of, actions is important to the analysis of the enactment of the discourse of change in this study. Perhaps most importantly in working with social media networks in the age of 'fake news,' sensemaking offers a frame of analysis that looks at actions and beliefs as driven by plausibility, not accuracy.

As text emerged from the social networks in these three case studies, I employed tools of discourse analysis to the content. Guided by Linda Putnam's (2005, p. 28) principles for conducting discourse analysis, I started with the four principles she proposed: (1) Let the text and context talk to you, (2) work back and forth between the text and the concepts, (3) look for inconsistencies, ironies or unexpected occurrences and (4) dispute your own interpretation and explanation. Although these elements provide an appropriate introduction to the analysis, they do not, as described earlier, reflect the central interest in power and privilege required by a critical analysis. Therefore, this research incorporates the work of Van Dijk (1993) and Phillips and Hardy (2002) to build on Putnam's model explicitly, to add a critical focus. The revised principles reflect this as:

1   Let the text and context talk to you; identify language and power and how these elements are privileged in the context of their production.
2   Work back and forth between the text and the concepts, reflecting the use of power, privilege and access to discourse which inform broader knowledge/power relationships.
3   Look for inconsistencies, ironies or unexpected occurrences, particularly language that silences other perspectives and marginalizes groups or individuals.
4   Dispute your own interpretation and explanation with attention to reflexivity that acknowledges the researcher's own sensemaking and participation in the production of discourse.

These revised principles served to establish signposts for the application of the analytic framework of CSM, which provided a lens to address individual agency. Critical sensemaking acknowledges that individuals make sense differently of the same text, experience, language or event. Although discourse analysis can accommodate this outcome, it is not equipped to draw out the explicit process by which individuals create elements of the narratives they share as meaningful.

The signposts described earlier facilitated the research process by ensuring that elements of the narratives that would be privileged through the application of CSM were identified in a manner that was consistent with a reflexive, dynamic and critical approach. As this study endeavored to maintain a process-focused, agency-centered analysis, these principles also established the guidelines for how language which emerged from the social networks would be privileged in the study and ultimately how individual sensemaking experiences would be privileged in a study of the process of change. A description of how these signposts were applied follows:

Text and context

The first step in analyzing the text from social media was to become immersed in the content of the text and identify elements of the formative context and related discourse that might represent themes or patterns. Emergent themes reflected elements such as examples of language used in relation to identity, lived experiences with organizational identities, rationalizations of organizational values and identities, and explanations of organizational identity statements. Consistent with the critical focus of this research, the analysis paid specific attention to descriptions of "the social practices associated with the applications of disciplinary techniques, individuals' reactions in terms of compliance or resistance, and implications for the constitution of identity" (Phillips & Hardy, 2002, p. 26).

In the application of the CSM framework to this analysis, the focus on text and context provided insight into the formative context and organizational rules which inform individual sensemaking. By integrating a critical approach with the analysis of the sensemaking context, pluralities of discourse began to emerge alongside organizational (and individual) narratives of identity. Ultimately, this method provided insight into what would emerge as dominant and/or competing understandings of identity throughout the network.

With regard to the visual text which emerged from the data, the nodes and edges within the networks were analyzed for context. Specifically, the direction and flow of information between members of the network, the relative centrality of the organization to the network and the location of influencers identified as nodes that engaged in a significant degree of two-way communication with others in the network. This context allowed me to see the speed and scope of the transfer of information across the network, the control of message content from the source (usually the organization) within this network, and the frequency of engagement within the network as ideas and identities were shared.

Work back and forth between the text and the concepts

Working back and forth between the text and the concepts keeps inferences about discourse patterns close to the observations of the data (Putnam, 2005, p. 29). At this point in the analysis, I was concerned with moving beyond an analysis of the language reflected at the local site of identity construction, the organization, and connecting the themes which had emerged to a broader understanding of organizational identity. This focus served to locate the language of identity represented at the local level within the broader discourse that defined organizational identity operating at a socio-cultural level. As a result, societal level discourses of regulation and control are central to this understanding of how individuals enact identity in organizations.

From a perspective of CSM, this assessment of the broader discursive environment highlights processes of identity construction, both for organizations and for individuals. This was reflected in descriptions of identities adopted by individuals (as 'good' employees or as 'warriors' for change, for example). When analyzed from the perspective of critical sensemaking, identity construction and plausibility play a significant role in the link between 'concepts' as macro-level discourse and individual sensemaking.

Look for inconsistencies, ironies or unexpected occurrences

Putnam (2005, p. 29) describes inconsistencies as "contradictions that appear in the text and call for the researcher to question the data." These presented opportunities for me to question my analysis and address puzzles presented in the data.

Dispute your own interpretation and explanation

In this final guiding principle Putnam (2005, p. 29) points out that "discourse analysts need to make decisions based on coherence among analytic schemes, evidence drawn from the texts, and interpretations that resonate with the situation." In the application of CSM, I adopted an approach of questioning interpretations in an effort to eliminate explanations that were either too disconnected from the identities presented, or did not resonate with insight drawn from other sources, the context of the research sites, or the theoretical framework of the study. This principle also served to illustrate the reflexive nature of the analysis, and challenged me to acknowledge my own role in the production of this study.

In the following chapters I will apply this approach to three specific case studies in an effort to surface processes of organizational identity construction from a critical perspective within the social media environment.

5 Plausibility, authenticity and collective enactment

From a CMS perspective, discursive power and legitimation of meaning are key components of the formative context in which sensemaking happens. These forces influence the plausibility of meaning and restrict or inform the range of possible meanings that individuals and organizations may accept as 'true.' In this chapter, I will discuss plausibility as reflected in the rhetorical strategies and practices of organizations in the process of constructing their identities.

The connection between legitimation and plausibility is often constructed communicatively through a process of authentication. What is the authentic or 'real truth' in terms of identity construction through social media? As discussed in earlier chapters, the CCO perspective does not essentialize the organization (nor the individual) as fixed. In this understanding of organizations as fluid, the problem of authenticity becomes elusive in the digital media environment. When we discussed the importance of plausibility previously as a component of the sensemaking process, the issue of ethics was not considered. Yet, the ethical representation of self remains a preoccupation within digital communication.

Authenticity

First, let's tackle the issue of authenticity as it relates to identity construction. Understandings of authenticity, as illustrated by Gaden and Dumitrica (2014) have changed over time. They point out that "thinkers like Montesquieu and Rousseau were concerned with imagining a new form of engagement with the world, where authenticity becomes the basis for an ethic of leading a virtuous life (Berman, 1970)" (p. 2). To live an authentic life was seen as both being true to oneself, and also engaging in a form of society where democratic process made it possible for one to live one's own authentic life, while respecting the rights of others to do the same. It was a balance between self-actualization and respect for boundaries that allowed others to live their authentic lives. This balance required a democratic engagement, respect for diverse perspectives and, as such, multivocal sensemaking. Thus, the formative context within which sensemaking could occur offered a range of possibilities which were constrained by the requirement to address both individual needs, and respect for space for others to pursue their own authentic selves at the same time.

Gaden and Dumitrica (2014) make the point that these earlier understandings of authenticity as requiring a type of participative, collaborative approach have been eroded to a narrower view of authenticity within the contemporary social media environment. The sheer volume of content available through social media has shifted the focus on authenticity to one of creating distinctiveness. Authenticity is seen as self-focused, as a mode of self-discovery or a rhetorical strategy to communicatively construct oneself as authentic within a sea of other voices. The plausibility of an authentic self is now more about constructing oneself as distinct from the noise of communication, and less about engagement. Likewise, concerns of morality and the authentically moral life have faded to the background in an effort to stake out distinctive individual space within the new media sphere.

As we expand this discussion to include not just an individual ethic of the authentic self but to organizations as well, the focus on authenticity begins to further shift from a personal ethic to lead a virtuous life, to a management or marketing strategy where organizations carve out space within the polyphonic environment of digital communication. The objective of that strategy is not so much concerned with the virtuous life of the organization but the creation of a distinctive voice in a crowded marketplace. This move is reflected as a shift away from the authentic engagement or democratization of organizational communication, and more toward the amplification of a distinctive organizational voice.

Although identities are constructed across a variety of social media platforms, the question of authenticity is perhaps most central to the use of micro-blogging or weblog (blogging) technologies. Blogging as a digital form emerged essentially as a forum for authentic communication, as individuals and organizations were to share their 'real lives' or day to day experiences – a kind of journaling. The term blogging was coined by Jorn Barger in 1997, and referred to weblogs or logs which were produced by web users itemizing websites of interest and providing minimum commentary. With the advent of accessible blogging software, the interest in blogs exploded and individuals began to incorporate blogging as communicative tools to present their own 'authentic' voice within a sea of commercialization and advertising (Gaden & Dumitrica, 2014). Authenticity in this context was seen as independence from a sponsor or advertiser, and the individual perspective (uninfluenced by others' agendas) of the author.

Blogging is also experienced by some individuals as a form of therapy (Gaden & Dumitrica, 2014, p. 6), where individuals enact sensemaking through their blog posts as they work through their own understandings of issues or experiences in a kind of self-reflection. This approach very much reflects the sensemaking recipe, "How can I know what I think until I see what I say?" (Westwood & Clegg, 2009, p. 193) that Weick has used to explain the process of enacting meaning through communication.

This same focus on authenticity can be applied to micro-blogging, as well as the 'larger' form. For example, the work of Sergi and Bonneau (2016) looks at how narratives of work experience can provide insights into the sensemaking process of organization. In their research on working out loud (WOL), "defined as a process of narrating work during the course of its realization" (p. 378), they investigate the way in which previously hidden processes of sensemaking are now revealed through social media interactions which allow for the authentic narration of an ongoing and social sensemaking process. They emphasize that WOL provides a unique set of circumstances through which to observe this process because the nature of this communication requires that the communication is informal and not specifically bounded by any one specific audience. The form of enactment of this sensemaking, in the case of their study of WOL on Twitter experienced as tweets, can take a written and conversational form, and, I suggest here that it can also encompass visual components and links to contextual material that may represent the work process in more detail, i.e. videos, graphics, etc.

Cooren's work (i.e. Cooren, 2004, 2012) within the Montreal School of CCO theory emphasizes the point that communicating is a hybrid activity which serves to share agency in the constitution of organizations between humans, and other abstract elements called 'figures.' Drawing on this approach to CCO, the work of Sergi and Bonneau (2016) suggests that this combination of actors, both human and non-human, contributes to the stabilization of organization even as it is constantly in creation through the production and assembly of communication over time. This perspective provides a useful lens through which to observe the ongoing conversation of organizing which persists across organizational members, technologies, elements and texts.

Working out loud, blogs and tweets can all arguably provide examples of authentic communication from the perspective of actual lived experience from 'real life.' None of them are necessarily concerned with the ethic of living a morally authentic life. In these cases, it appears more so that authentic equates to 'unscripted,' as opposed to any deeper analysis. Although this shift away from historical understandings of authenticity may be problematic in some ways, these unscripted accounts of sensemaking provide useful examples of enacted meaning both individually and on a large scale of organization.

Enacted sensemaking

Enacted sensemaking in the case of social media use such as blogs or tweets, can be seen as both a probing of context for plausible explanations and a production of narratives through which to crystalize sensemaking by enacting meaning. The way in which individuals and organizations come to privilege some narratives as plausible, and discard others, is an important part of the process. Weick emphasizes that this is not a straightforward process, and that plausibility in collective sensemaking must also relate to the concept of trust. In his work on organizational tragedy, Weick suggests that:

> a vocabulary of sensemaking might start with these basics:
>
>> Disorder + confusion + insecurity = trouble.
>> Trouble + thinking = sensemaking.
>> Probing for plausible stories that explain trouble = enacted sensemaking.
>> (Weick, 2010, p. 543)

As sensemaking occurs around junctures or shocks to organizational routines, Weick posits that issues of trust come to the forefront during organizational crisis. In those instances, the questions of who we are (identity) and how we do things (culture) are evaluated as organizational members search for plausible understandings of the situation.

In order for organizational members to engage in the positive sensemaking that is required in times of organizational crisis, processes of communication have to be established well in advance. Weick reminds us that how individuals and organizations make sense of their environments relies heavily on what went before. From that perspective, trust must be established in order for plausible alternatives presented by others to be accepted and enacted. Specifically:

> People need to trust the reports of others and be willing to base their beliefs and actions on them.
> People have to be trustworthy observers and report honestly so that others can use their observations in coming to valid beliefs.
> People have to maintain self-respect, which means they have to respect their own perceptions and beliefs, and seek to integrate them with the reports of others without belittling either the others or themselves.
> (Weick, 2003, p. 75)

Thus, a collective enactment of sensemaking hinges as much on the properties of retrospection and social engagement in this ongoing process as individuals draw on their prior experiences with communication, plausibility and trust.

Although the concept of collective enactment of meaning is often understood to reflect a high degree of agency, this is not necessarily the case. From a CSM perspective, enactment, whether individual or collective, is constrained by the context in which it exists. Only a specific range of options are available to those doing the sensemaking – and as such only a limited number of options may be enacted. In fact, the opportunities for an individual to influence collective sensemaking within an organization might actually be quite limited.

Enactment in this sense refers to any action that makes real, so to speak, the constructed meaning. This includes speaking aloud, writing, as well as the tangible actions that are visible throughout the organization. Social media emerge in this discussion as key sites of enactment not only because the engagement with social media technology may facilitate activities, such as organizing, which reflects this collective action. It is also important to recognize that the actual production of content across social media platforms provides opportunity for enacted sensemaking. As Weick points out in (Westwood & Clegg, 2009, p. 193):

> Many discussions of enactment have little to say about the stuff of organization, by which I mean the technology, artifacts and other material forms that are so important to people like Latour and Czarniawska. . . . Writing and editing and reading are major pastimes in organizational life that enact prominent environments. And yet they are invisible in many discussions of enactment.

To that end, the ways in which social media content are both consumed and produced enact sensemaking and reinforce organizing within the network. In today's social media environment, we see changes occurring in terms of language being used, the construction of meaning, the symbolic construction of semiotic communication, etc. For example, the communication of content through the use of emjois and emoticon symbols through text and online communication. These elements of sensemaking achieve durability as artifacts of communication, but also occur in processes of interpretation and construction of meaning.

The advent of social media has hyper-focused our attention on writing and reading, albeit the context in which these happen has certainly changed. And at the same time the production of text has expanded to include photos, videos, images, etc., all of which convey meaning on different levels. The infinite volume of this material has also placed a renewed focus on the sensemaking property of extracted cues. The ways in which cues are extracted, or how some social media messages surface as meaningful while others do not, is central to how the boundaries of plausible alternatives are established.

From a CCO perspective, this connection between the micro-level production of individual communication through tweets, blogs, photos, etc., and the macro-level production of organizational identity work in tandem to create an interconnected, and arguably self-sustaining, network of communication that constitutes an organization, and ultimately, a social order of organizations within society. Seidl and Becker (2006), as cited in Blaschke et al., 2012, p. 880), point to CCO theory as a "new response to the challenge of reconciling the micro level of local communication, the meso level of the organization, and the macro level of society." Likewise, Blaschke et al. (2012), emphasize that "sequences of communication events unfold into communication episodes, which in turn recursively interlock" and form organizational structures constituted through communication processes. They further describe the formation of macro-level contexts by highlighting that "organizational communication draws on institutionalized templates of communication that society holds in stock (Cooren & Fairhurst, 2009; Seidl, 2007; Taylor, Cooren, Giroux, & Robichaud, 1996)" (as cited in Blaschke et al., 2012, p. 880). CSM also addresses the relationship between agency and individual which Weick describes as an interdependency in which micro level processes and routines shape the outcomes of macro level organizing (Weick et al., 2005). In this way, Weick describes individuals as organizing through processes of enactment, individually and collectively creating scripts and institutions that ultimately act to constrain them.

At the same time it is important to maintain some optimism about the potential of social media to allow for alternative sensemaking and to make change. Our understanding of these technologies from a CCO perspective may create space for different ways of knowing and seeing meaning as it is both produced by and productive of the broader formative context. As Blaschke et al. (2012) assert, the CCO perspective offers "a new perspective on the fundamentally contested character of meaning that explains why the scope of managerial control over the communicative practices that constitute an organization is limited (Fairhurst, 2008; Luhmann, 2003)" (p. 880).

Previously inaccessible ways of enacting meaning, including these enhanced and accelerated modes of writing and reading, have broadened the field somewhat and may encourage more frequent junctures, or challenges to routine sensemaking. As Paul Mason (2012) tells us "one fact is clear: people know more than they used to . . . they have greater and more instant access to knowledge, and reliable ways of countering disinformation. Why should a revolution in knowledge and technology not be producing an equally dramatic – albeit diametrically opposite – change in human behaviour?" (Mason 2012, p. 147 cited in Gerbaudo, 2012, p. 7).

Given the constraints discussed previously, a democratization of social media remains problematic. Nevertheless, there do seem to be some changes in terms of how individuals access information, and how they are motivated to enact it. As Kavada (2015) points out, we need to "reframe collective action as being constituted by a set of communication practices involving the crossing of boundaries from the private to the public realm (Flanagin et al., 2006)."

As boundaries are crossed between public and private, or between micro- and macro-level contexts, a number of forms of collective identity construction have emerged. These range from social activism through phenomenon such as the Occupy movement, to movements of revolution and/or nationalism in such forms as the Arab Spring. In the last decade or so, the emergence of crowdsourcing, and alternatively, crowdfunding, has presented a collective form of capitalism. These alternative forms of, arguably, democratized capitalism have rapidly gained legitimacy as authentic forms of engagement within an otherwise exclusively capitalist environment. However, this potential is tempered by the constrained nature of the context in which even these newer arrangements of enacted communication occur.

Fragmentation and legitimation

Kent and Taylor's (2014) work on the future of social media in public relations provided six emergent themes requiring our attention in the digital media age. These themes were identified through a Delphi technique with a panel of public relations experts who, among other things, highlighted two contradictory elements which in some ways define the challenge of social media authenticity and collective sensemaking. The first is a tendency toward fragmentation, the second is a tendency toward collaboration with like-minded individuals. Fragmentation and collaboration define two ends of the social media spectrum, and these two approaches can work both for and against processes of legitimation. Fragmentation is understood by Kent and Taylor (2014) as a process of dissociation from relationships as communication is increasingly shared in asynchronous environments. This circumstance is compounded by the fact that individuals enrolled in networks through social media are often engaged with such large numbers of 'friends' or 'followers' that the sheer volume of people engaged in any given conversation makes it impossible for deep communication or relationship building. Further complicating this situation, and related to the next challenge, is the likelihood of individuals who express an opposing view to others in the network to be blocked or jettisoned from the conversation. The convergence of technological limitations and limited 'real' human interactions leads to a fragmented communication environment where individuals are isolated into silos from the broader public sphere.

As the range of possible meanings is narrowed within the formative context of CSM, fewer plausible alternatives exist. These possibilities begin to then reinforce one another, until counter narratives, or multivocal perspectives are not only viewed as implausible, they simply don't exist in the conversation. As Weick explains, the scripts that individuals enact (collectively) to define the *who we are*, as well as *how things are done here*, ultimately can serve to constrain the sensemaking which follows by forcing boundaries to the routine. In the digital media environment, this effect is magnified.

The second theme, collaboration, speaks to both the promise of democratization through social media, and the further entrenchment of echo chambers hosting narrowed conversations which persist in separate streams.

> As the Internet grows more sophisticated, it is creating new threats to democracy. Social media companies such as Facebook can sort us ever more efficiently into groups of the like-minded, creating echo chambers

that amplify our views. It's no accident that on some occasions, people of different political views cannot even understand one another. It's also no surprise that terrorist groups have been able to exploit social media to deadly effect. Welcome to the age of #*Republic*.

(Sunstein, 2018)

The construction of echo chambers or silos in which sensemaking is increasingly limited is facilitated by processes of human communication which search to limit challenge and change and work with only comfortable or routine understandings of the world. The social media landscape today is also very much defined by the work of machines, which are programmed to accelerate that same process, and provide us alternatives that serve to reinforce, not challenge, our sensemaking.

Framing

Both of these trends, fragmentation and collaboration, are concerns of a growing literature on framing in social media. Framing has grown to be one of the most researched areas of media scholarship over the past two decades (Cacciatore, Scheufele, & Iyengar, 2016). Nevertheless, this increase in interest on framing has not resulted in clarification of either what framing is or how the concept can be applied to advance our understanding of the theory behind media framing (Tewksbury & Scheufele, 2007).

Constraints to the range of sensemaking alternatives have always been a central question within scholarship on media framing. Broadly speaking, from a social media perspective framing defines the sensemaking processes which inform the production and consumption of social media content.

That being said, there are a number of approaches to framing in the literature. As Cacciatore et al. (2016, p. 8) summarize in their work entitled "The end of Framing as we know it":

> Druckman (2001), for instance, listed no fewer than seven definitions of the concept. These range from frames as 'principles of organization' (Goffman, 1974, p. 10) to frames as 'principles of selection, emphasis, and presentation' (Gitlin, 1980, p. 6). Sweetser and Fauconnier (1996) defined frames as 'structured understandings of the way aspects of the world function' (p. 5), whereas Capella and Jamieson (1997) offered a definition more directly tied to journalism, arguing that framing is the manner in which a 'story is written or produced.'
>
> (p. 39)

These diverse and somewhat fluid understandings of framing reflected in the literature offer an unclear picture of how sensemaking occurs using a framing approach. The different conceptual models available to scholars working with media framing address a range of interpretations; however,

I suggest here that the foundational and enduring components which continue to resonate with those interested in Framing are essentially those of CSM and consistent as well with CCO. This is consistent at a foundational level with Entman's early definition of frames as structures that serve to "highlight some bits of information about an item that is the subject of a communication, thereby elevating them in salience" (Entman, 1993, p. 53).

Weick has long held that the function of sensemaking is to establish and/ or maintain routine around 'the way things are done.' As Maitlis (2010) points out,

> Central to the development of plausible meanings is the bracketing of cues from the environment, and the interpretation of those cues based on salient frames. Sensemaking is thus about connecting cues and frames to create an account of what is going on.
>
> (p. 552)

It is a communicative process of making meaning from within chaos and disorder. There are strong connections at this very fundamental level with Goffman's (1974) principles of organization, or Gitlin's (1980) principles of selection, emphasis and presentation. In essence these reflect elements of extracting cues, retrospection and enacted sensemaking, all within a formative context which 'frames,' if you will, the larger picture and constrains the range of possible alternatives which may be presented.

In order to make connections between work on sensemaking and the categories of framing discussed in the literature I will use the approach of Cacciatore et al. (2016) and divide the main trends into the two streams of equivalency framing (i.e. Kahneman & Egan, 2011; Druckman, 2001) and emphasis framing (Iyengar, 2005).

Equivalency framing refers in broad terms to those definitions of framing concerned with how information is provided, the words and phrases selected, and the resulting 'equivalency effect' (Cacciatore et al., 2016). This approach is rooted in psychology and focuses on variations in how information is presented as opposed to what information is provided. Kahneman (2003) describes this process as "reference dependent" (p. 459) in that the choice an individual sensemaking will select is dependent upon the contextual information provided in the way it is communicated. As Cacciatore et al. (2016) summarize, this work "has been labeled equivalency framing because it relies upon different but logically equivalent words or phrases to produce the framing effect (Druckman, 2001)" (p. 10).

The question of 'how' choice is presented reflects a central concern within CSM scholarship. This is the point at which key elements of the sensemaking properties are influenced or emphasized by the power effects of the formative context in which they operate. Helms Mills (2003) emphasizes that all options or all available alternatives to the construction of sensemaking narratives are not universally available to all sensemakers. The constraints around what is an available option is most often characterized within acceptance, or not, of any given sensemaking alternative as plausible for its audience.

The idea that perception is 'reference dependent' as described previously once again highlights the connection between the willingness of sensemakers to accept a particular narrative as plausible as highly dependent on the reference of the individual sensemaker. It must resonate with retrospection, the individual's past experience; with other cues in the environment; with the extraction of these supporting cues; and as illustrated in a number of CSM studies, with the individual or organization extracting those cues on behalf of the sensemaker.

In my work with CCO and CSM, I am drawing principally from the sociological tradition of framing. This approach approaches sensemaking as a way of understanding the ways in which individuals make sense of the everyday world through the social construction of meaning. (Ferree, Gamson, Gerhards, & Rucht, 2002). My contention here is that discursive strategies traditionally understood as frames have transformed in the social media context to strategies of legitimation which privilege some narratives of sensemaking within an extremely crowded media landscape. This view is more or less consistent with the second category of framing which I refer to here as emphasis framing.

Emphasis framing differs from equivalence framing in that it is concerned beyond how the information is presented into the domain of what is presented (Cacciatore et al., 2016). The selection of 'facts,' details and context move this type of framing past the application of 'logically equivalent information' and into the actual construction of sensemaking through privileging of some sensemaking alternatives, or narratives, above others. Thus, this category of framing has been labeled emphasis framing as the discursive process at work here serves to emphasize one narrative, or one argument, over others in the framing of plausible meanings. Druckman argues that "(emphasis) framing effect is said to occur when, in the course of describing an issue or event, a speaker's emphasis on a subset of potentially relevant considerations causes individuals to focus on these considerations when constructing their opinions" (2001, p. 1042).

Historically, emphasis framing has been the more widely used approach to framing scholarship within the communication literature. And it includes a variety of types of research within its boundaries, including thematic framing. "The thematic frame places an issue in some general context and usually takes the form of an in-depth, 'backgrounder' report" (Iyengar, 2005, p. 6).

As Entman (1993) asserts,

> Although both equivalency and emphasis framing effects cause individuals to focus on certain aspects of an issue over others, the information subsets presented in emphasis framing are not logically identical to one another. Nelson, Oxley and Clawson (1997) argue that issue frames tell

people how to weight the often conflicting considerations that we face on a daily basis. Frames, therefore, have the best possibility to affect public opinion when emphasizing a subset of different and potentially relevant considerations.

(p. 182)

Sniderman and Theriault (2004) further illustrate this point by illustrating that when

government spending for the poor is framed as enhancing the chance that poor people can get ahead, individuals tend to support increased spending. However, when such government spending is framed as increasing taxes, individuals tend to oppose government spending to help the poor. Once again, these examples show that emphasizing certain considerations over others can produce different opinions on the same issue.

(p. 143)

This category also includes a variety of theoretical concepts which cover some diverse ground in terms of what a frame is, and how it functions. For example, the conceptualization of frames as scripts or schemas has been identified by a number of scholars (Fiske & Taylor, 1991; Markus & Zajonc, 1985; Rumelhart, 1984; Schank & Abelson, 1977). This same conceptualization of sensemaking as a kind of script fits with the view of a frame as a tool to help individual sensemakers cope with the high volume of information they encounter in an ongoing way (Wicks, 1992). This conceptualization is not dissimilar from Weick's (1995) view of the sensemaking property of extracted cues, again emphasizing how individuals must privilege and select some cues over others within a cluttered environment and within a broad formative context. Along those same lines, Minsky (1975) provides a definition of a frame as a cognitive template or structure used to organize information in the mind (Cacciatore et al., 2016).

The trend of collaboration highlighted by Kent and Taylor cautions us to the ways in which social media platforms can facilitate framing of information for a like-minded audience, resulting in echo chambers where we make sense of information within a narrowly constrained range of alternatives that fit our existing values or experiences. Cacciatore et al. (2016) describe this process from a framing perspective as reflecting preference-based models, and relate these to the scholarship on media effects. They contend that "rapidly changing media environments and evolving audience behaviors within these environments . . . have begun to push into . . . media effects research: preference-based effects models" (p. 18).

Scholarship in this area suggests that media effects will ultimately become increasingly limited in social media environments, as the fragmented nature of online audiences and the highly selective process of extracting cues in this environment unfold. Essentially, new media technologies continue to be more and more adept at putting together audiences with information that matches up with their pre-existing beliefs. Therefore, the opportunity for media to influence or challenge meaning within this group is less and less apparent (Bennett & Iyengar, 2008). Social media framing, therefore, may serve only to reinforce existing beliefs and further isolate individuals from multivocal sensemaking in an authentic (democratic) sense.

This concern is amplified in the literature by communication scholars whose work draws attention to emergent digital tools such as aggregators, machine-learning models, search engines and the like which have the potential to create 'filter bubbles' (Pariser, 2011). These are described as occurring when computer-generated algorithms automatically recommend content with which the recipient is likely to agree, thus reinforcing existing preferences and limiting polyvonic communication. Pariser (2011, p. 5) states

> The new generation of internet filters looks at the things you seem to like – the actual things you've done, or the things people like you like – and tries to extrapolate . . . who you are and what you'll do and want next.

Messing and Westwood (2012) describe the workings of a particular algorithm.

> "Recent attention has also been directed at what Facebook calls EdgeRank (Facebook, 2010), an algorithm that the company employs that determines with whom one most frequently interacts in order to determine whose content appears in that friend's news feed. Such algorithms can serve to increase homophily because the more one clicks on content posted by similar individuals, the more likely that content posted from such individuals is likely to appear in their news feeds.
>
> (p. 7)

This in turn may reinforce the properties of retrospective, social and ongoing sensemaking. As Weick (1995) emphasizes, sensemaking must resonate with the individual's past experiences. It is also constructed socially, through engagement with other sensemakers on an ongoing basis. Sensemaking doesn't stop at a fixed point in the process. It continues in an ongoing fashion until meaning is established and becomes routine. As social media technologies work to reinforce the plausibility and social acceptability of a given narrative, the more likely it is to become a routine or script within the network. This process also harkens back to Weick's (1996) emphasis on the importance of micro-level processes, and the ways in which the organizing within a defined social network, for example, may reflect the mirror effects of that organizing on a macro-level as well.

Furthermore, individuals appear more willing to share, like or recommend information to their social media networks if they agree with the content involved. This could further constrain the range of sensemaking alternatives available as individuals begin to self-select their own formative contexts, and within these, the range of narratives deemed plausible. What does this mean for public relations scholars concerned with engagement around organizational identity? Kent (2013) addresses both the potential and the limitations of social media for public relations practitioners interested in engagement, suggesting that one of the key components of the relationship between democracy and public communication is the role of the gatekeeper. "Without the aid of credible gatekeepers and media professionals, democracy is hobbled, just as it is by having its media controlled by only five mega-corporations" (p. 338). He asserts that the previous model of public relations access to mass audiences was problematic due to the convergence of media outlets closely aligned with capitalist interests. In the 1990s, the internet emerged and this bottleneck to information access was opened up. However, this development also brought the complication of the role of the gatekeeper. In the move away from mainstream media, the role of the editor or journalist is less central. Kent reminds us that in the absence of these "professional gatekeepers who made editorial decisions, citizens have increasingly come to rely on a greater diversity of news sources (some more credible than others), and more idiosyncratic voices that appeal to individual citizens' unique interests" (p. 338). This caution in some ways brings us back to the question of extracted cues. Is there a role for public relations practitioners as information gatekeepers, or must we rely on the network itself to select and extract the most plausible (not necessarily most accurate) cues?

In the examples that follow we will explore some of the constraints described earlier, but also some of the ways that social media networks have actually transcended the limitations of constrained sensemaking to utilize that potential for engagement which may allow for alternative voices. The grip of the echo chamber may not, in fact, be as all-encompassing as predicted. Although the long-term impact of the rapid expansion of artificial intelligence within public communication is not yet fully known, some scholars continue to predict that the potential for democratic engagement is still a possibility.

For example, Messing and Westwood (2012) provide research on the richness of cues available for individual sensemaking through social media. They contend that there are more and richer cues now available through social media platforms than through other information selection processes in the form of likes, shares, re-tweets etc. This direct endorsement from members of the social network is a powerful tool in the extraction of cues and therefore privileging of information for consumption. In their study of recommender traits on content selection they find that the propensity of individuals to consume content recommended by 'friends' can mitigate against the limitations of self-selection based on source. In cases where individuals are part of broad and diverse networks, information which is surfaced by these contacts may ultimately result in more diverse opinions and information being consumed.

Flaxman, Goel, and Rao (2016) point to the work of Benkler (2006) and others (Obendorf, Herder Eelco, & Matthias, 2007; Goel, Hofman, & Sirer, 2012) as they suggest that technologies like search engines and social media networks may reduce ideological segregation as a result of increased choice and the interconnections of networks across platforms. Flaxman et al. conclude in their study that actually the online information consumption patterns of participants in the study more or less mirrored their offline consumption. For example, individuals tended to follow the website or social network reporting of the same media outlets that they would follow offline. Nevertheless, in the online environment there was greater potential for these individuals to become exposed to alternative opinions and information as networks intersected across platforms.

In their work connecting the approaches of framing and sensemaking, Fiss and Hirsch (2005) emphasize that the context in which sensemaking happens is as important as the construction of the narrative or message itself. "Connecting framing and sensemaking better enables us to examine how structural factors prompt and bound discursive processes, affecting when and where frame contests emerge" (Fiss & Hirsch, 2005, p. 29) From this perspective, the importance of shocks or junctures in the sensemaking process can help to identify and define the emergence of frames. As these frames are constructed, sensemaking properties come into focus.

As our understanding of what framing involves becomes more diversified in the media landscape, the technologies through which these frames are constructed are becoming more fragmented and complex. Social media platforms, as discussed in previous chapters, have not only transformed the way information can be shared with audiences, but in fact, who the audiences are, and what their relationship with the information should be. Ultimately, in the social media context, sensemakers are responsible for 'setting' their own frames, extracting their own cues (within technological and sociopolitical constraints) and constructing multiple identities.

While we pull together both the CCO and the CSM frameworks in this work to provide a fuller context through which to understand how some sensemaking alternatives are privileged over others, we see that the processes of sensemaking themselves engage in a form of framing at the micro-level, while the formative context in which they operate constructs a macro-level framing that operates on a broader, discursive level. It is this relationship that I attempt to clarify in the following chapters as we see the tenets of CCO and CSM working at levels of both individual agency, as in the case of resistance to dominant narratives, and at the level of organization, on local and global levels.

6 Crowdfunding – collective organizing and virtual identities

The term 'crowdsourcing' refers to an emergent form of social media organizing which includes a wide variety of outcomes and practices. The term itself was coined by Jeff Howe as a contraction of the words "crowd" and "outsourcing" in the June 2006 edition of *Wired* (Howe, 2006a). The earliest forms of this phenomenon appear to have their origins in the late 1990s where the term emerged to describe a type of outsourcing initiated by corporations looking to reduce costs (Thurlow & Yue, 2013). For the most part this outsourcing was related to data gathering, market research focus groups and the desire to de-centralize call-center type functions so that stakeholders would have a channel to communicate with the company directly (Howe, 2006a).

An early example of crowdsourcing was identified by Schenk and Guittard (2009) describing an initiative developed by Eli Lilly, an American multinational pharmaceutical company. In 1998, Eli Lilly pioneered a crowd-outsourcing project called InnoCentive, a platform that essentially allowed consumers to provide feedback to the corporation on their products. Since that time, crowdsourcing has exploded as both a tool of corporate cost-cutting and a method for other forms of organization to form, converge or resist established capitalist structures. The academic literature to date has only recently begun to develop a body of work on forms of crowdsourcing, and within the public relations literature specifically, the focus tends to be on crowdfunding (Schenk & Guittard, 2011). In contrast, the professional literature has extensive coverage of the growth of this approach over the past decade. And dozens of blogs are dedicated to the topic (e.g. http://crowdsourcing.typepad.com) (Schenk & Guittard, 2009, p. 3).

As crowdsourcing has expanded in its application in recent years, this diversity has led to a blurring of the boundaries of its definition. At this point, crowdsourcing may be "identified virtually with any type of internet-based collaborative activity, such as co-creation or user innovation" (Estellés-Arolas & González-Ladrón-de-Guevara, 2012, abstract). This has resulted in varied and sometimes conflicting understandings of the phenomenon. As we discuss crowdsourcing here, I will draw on Jeff Howe's (2006b) definition:

> the act of a company or institution taking a function once performed by employees and outsourcing it to an undefined (and generally large)

network of people in the form of an open call. This can take the form of peer-production (when the job is performed collaboratively), but is also often undertaken by sole individuals. The crucial prerequisite is the use of the open call format and the large network of potential laborers (para. 4).

It is useful to acknowledge before discussing the current state of crowdsourcing that these types of relationships have a long history offline as well. Qiu (2013, p. 1) provides an example of John Taylor, a seventeenth-century poet, who persuaded about 1,650 readers to pledge money for his journey to Scotland on foot for a new book, The Pennyless Pilgrimage. Taylor promised to repay the pledgers with copies of the book. However, he apparently had trouble collecting on a number of the pledge commitments even up to a year later (Poyntz, 2011). Bannerman (2013) offers a list of examples including;

> Pepsodent held a jingle-writing contest advertised in *Life* magazine in 1950. Readers of Pepsodent's advertisement were invited to send in their jingles in a bid to win prizes, with the grand prize being $10,000 ('Pepsodent', 1950). The Canadian Broadcasting Corporation (CBC) crowdsourced a new Hockey Night in Canada theme song in 2008 after a dispute over payments for the rights to the classic theme originally commissioned from composer Dolores Claman (Hockey, 2010) (in Bannerman, 2013, p. 4).

Although these forms of social organizing around projects differ in approach, they contain a similar focus – crowdfunding (via social media or not) is based on the fact that people want be engaged with other people, ideas and projects that they like and that are close to them, emotionally or geographically. As Bannerman (2013) explains,

> The true significance of crowdsourcing and crowdfunding lies not just in their technological innovation, but also in the way they shift mindsets and realities around organizational possibility, potentially reinforcing and extending, or even altering, the traditional organization of cultural production (p. 9).

To that end, Howe (2009, p. 11) asserts that the "human behaviors technology engenders, especially the potential to weave the mass of humanity together into a thriving, infinitely powerful organism" is the ultimate potential of crowdsourcing. He views crowdfunding platforms as facilitating "the mobilization of ideas, the interconnection of funders with creators, the bringing together of ideas and resources, and new organizational possibilities" (Bannerman, 2013, p.10).

Some of the most popular crowdfunding platforms today include Kickstarter, GoFundMe, Indiegogo and Appbacker. There are many others, and new forms of organizing through this media continue to emerge. Typically, each platform has a specific purpose, for example, a platform called Kiva is a loan-based crowd-funded microcredit site. Qiu (2013) points out that the reward-based category is the largest by the number of platforms (Crowdsourcing.org, 2012), and one of the largest sites in this category is Kickstarter. "In 2012, US$320 million worth of contributions were made through Kickstarter, which constitutes over 10% of the total crowdfunding volume that year" (Qiu, 2013, p. 1).

Social activism and action

In many cases, the motivation behind crowdsourcing has a social action component. This can be realized in the form of seeking alternative approaches to traditional financing opportunities, or garnering support for social justice or community development initiatives. Crowdfunding happens exclusively through social media networks, and in many ways mirrors examples of social activism that are taking place through those same channels. As Kahn and Kellner (2004) point out, there has been a surge of grassroots movements attempting to carry out "globalization from below" in opposition to "the capitalist strategy of globalization-from-above" (p. 89). And the individuals and groups engaged in this type of activism are not necessarily the traditional activist organizations.

> As the virtual community theorist Howard Rheingold (2002) notes, advances in personal, mobile informational technology are providing rapidly the structural elements for the existence of fresh kinds of highly-informed, autonomous communities that coalesce around local lifestyle choices, global political demands, and everything in between.
>
> (Hammer & Kellner, 2009, p. 89)

In the following examples, we will take a look at two applications of crowdfunding strategies, one with a motivation designed to alleviate the challenge of lack of access to credit, and the other to engage communities in a social action endeavor. The first example, the Warehouse Expansion, was featured in a previous work on crowdfunding and communication (Thurlow & Yue, 2013). Since then, the same initiative has expanded to run two further projects and represents an example of an expanding wave of small businesses, entrepreneurial ventures which are resourced in a collective, technologically mediated fashion.

Warehouse expansion

One regional example of a very successful crowdfunding campaign comes from the Brooklyn Warehouse in Halifax. When traditional forms of financing a renovation and expansion were not accessible to the owners of this restaurant, they reached out through social media to launch a crowdfunding project. The owners made an arrangement with their landlord to share the costs of adding a porch front addition to the restaurant. Through crowdfunding, they set out to raise $30,000 in 60 days to cover their share of the costs. When the project closed in February 2012, they had engaged 116 backers and raised over $23,000 to result in 77.3% funding of the project.

As described in print media coverage of the project:

> Crowd-funding project is an alternative to conventional financing and a feel-good way for customers to pool their resources, support the restaurant's expansion and reap the rewards through good food. Donors can pitch in anywhere from $10 to $2,500 and will receive in turn an equally valued meal, company clothing or permanent recognition on a wall of supporters to be constructed in the Halifax restaurant.

Restaurant co-owner Leo Christakos said, "We were literally bursting at the seams and it was time for us to do something with our business." So they decided to replace the restaurant's summer patio with a permanent, all-season atrium and nearly double the seating capacity. He added, "The interest that we'd pay back to a bank and the interest that we're currently paying to our landlord – who has helped us fund the construction – is high, so instead of borrowing that money to fund it, we'd rather pay that back to our customers in good food and good taste."

It's meant to be a positive process and the feel-good aspect should be there.

"We're offering back good will and we're building a sense of community because the donor is becoming part of the process. They're making the decision to support what you're doing and they want to see you succeed" (Cosgrove, 2011). This media report highlights both the idea of joining an emerging community, but importantly also shows how the optimization of financial resources is part of the dialogue that enables such a community to emerge. This is not a private loan process, but rather an open and transparent discussion about resources needed for organizational growth and becoming part of something through the creation of meaning. If 'angel' investing is about people with money looking for investment opportunities, then this is about people having dialogue about the need for financing, making community and translating this into financial support.

We earlier linked crowdfunding, dialogue and certain types of social media usage. In the case of the Brooklyn Warehouse example we are investigating, we see evidence of such social media usage. Below is the blog post that launched the crowdfunding project, engaging participants through social media:

> "Hey!
> We're at it again. Changing all the rules.
> We are inviting you, the Fans of The Brooklyn Warehouse, to our crowdfunding blog with the hope that you can afford a small (or large)

donation in an effort to fund the patio expansion currently underway and in return, receive a nice tasty reward for your support.

(from the Brooklyn Warehouse blog at
http://brooklynwarehouse.ca/wordpress/?p=1400)

Not many people know about Crowdfunding so we've taken the time to explain how it works and what it's all about. One aspect about a successful crowdfunding campaign is that it must rely on you, not only to donate, but also to get the word out to others; it's basically word-of-mouth, which is how we built our business in the first place.

So, jump in and check out the campaign, see if any of the rewards fit your budget and appetite; and don't forget to donate! Follow the blog, make your comments or add a backer's post. Then, send the link as an invitation to people in your social network that you think would find this site, the rewards, or The Brooklyn Warehouse something worth looking at.

Check It Out! http://brooklynhfx.blogspot.com/p/about-this-project_17.html Thanks for your support!

Leo, George & the Crew

In this case, the crowdfunding project offered community members a chance to embrace a non- traditional response to raising capital. The social benefits of the project were as important as the value exchanged in terms of food for investments. This community-minded action reflects a growing dialogue on a larger scale in terms of 'Mainstreet versus Wallstreet.' Interestingly, the Brooklyn Warehouse also proposed some collective meals in response to requests from crowdfunding investors. In basic terms, individuals are interested in meeting and sharing a meal with others who participated in the project. This transference from social media, to a social gathering is an interesting development in the dialogue around this project.

In the case of the Brooklyn Warehouse, geographic community appears to be important. Many individuals posting on the blog indicated support for a local restaurant in their local community. However, engagement in a crowdfunding community does not necessarily require geographic proximity. In fact, one of the advantages of the medium involved is that distance doesn't matter.

Since this first experience with crowdfunding, the owners of the Brooklyn Warehouse have gone on to run another successful crowd-funded renovation of that restaurant, and most recently a third crowdfunding initiative for another eatery in the city called Battery Park. The emotional selling point for these campaigns for the owners is not just the micro-loans which fund the construction, but the tangible evidence that their customers believe in them. They describe this relationship as more of a community-building experience than an investment opportunity. (Nevertheless, the owners never lose sight of the fact that this is an economic transaction in the end. Their pitch to donors as they launch this latest campaign is: "we give more value, for example if you donate $100 to the campaign, we will give you more than $100 worth of goods and services. You get more for your money" http:// batterypark.ca/theproject/).

This third campaign raised over $35,000 (CDN). Although, the owners reported in their blog updates that engagement remained high:

> First, several backers actually contributed more than once; the practice being that they bought into more than one tier so they could give a gift to someone else . . . which is pretty cool! Additionally, some of these people are serial contributors, returning to the crowd from the previous Brooklyn Warehouse projects; obviously, satisfied customers, if not just people who know a good deal when they see one. They really get what this is all about, and know they are getting a great return with their contribution, in whatever form they decided to participate in and help out with financing this project in good taste.
>
> (Christakos, 2015, para. 2).

All three of these campaigns were enacted on social media, and communicated largely through a focused blog, micro-blogging and website-based messaging.

The next example of crowdfunding we will explore looks at the emergence and persistence of a global organization called the Awesome Foundation. This is an interesting global example of crowdfunding with a distinctly community focus. As opposed to the previous example which was motivated by a lack of access to credit, this example is important because it involves outsourcing of financing with an overarching goal not related to productivity or charity, areas which seem obvious matches for crowdfunding efforts. In the case of the Awesome Foundation, the motivation is about building a global community and, as stated in the organization's description "advancing the interest of awesome in the universe, $1000 at a time" (www. awesomefoundation.org/en/about_us)

The corporate website describes its core identity in the following way:

> The Awesome Foundation is an ever-growing worldwide community devoted to forwarding the interest of awesome in the universe. Created in the long hot summer days of 2009 in Boston, the Foundation distributes $1,000 grants, no strings attached, to projects and their creators. At each fully autonomous chapter, the money is pooled together from the coffers of ten or so self-organizing 'micro-trustees' and given up front in cash, check, or gold doubloons.

In terms of structure, each individual chapter in the organization operates entirely independently, and almost none of these have formally registered as organizations. Most chapters are defined within geographic boundaries, but several are organized along thematic lines. A small community of volunteers takes care of the global shared infrastructure which includes an online presence, a Twitter account and other social media platforms.

The Foundation describes itself to potential members as being distinctive, and works to identify itself as different from other non-profit initiatives.

> The Awesome Foundation isn't your average foundation. We're not a charity or a not-for-profit. We're a group of local citizens who simply believe that the world, and specifically our city, needs more awesome. And we're opening our own wallets to help make that happen. In total, there are 30 of us. Together, we are the Trustees of Awesome. Every month 10 Trustees get together and chip in $100 to form a grant of $1,000. Our groups of 10 rotate every month so that each of us gets to help make awesome happen four times a year.

The organization is very much focused on local organizing, and as the corporate website states, they are organized 'very loosely.' The Awesome chapter in Sydney, Australia, for example, encourages projects such as:

> We love turning awesome thoughts into awesome deeds in this awesome city of ours*.
>
> Like the other chapters, every month we award a $1,000 no-strings-attached grant to the most awesome application**.
>
> Previous recipients of an Awesome Foundation Sydney grant include: a project to develop the world's smallest patch synthesizer, the Green Bans Art Walk, the Oxford Street Design Store and Exhibition, pop up ping pong in inner Sydney, hula hoop classes and Physique, a weekly 80s themed aerobics night.
>
> *Applications which focus on making Sydney a more awesome place are our favourite kind, please keep that in mind!.
>
> (Awesome Sydney)

The Moscow chapter also emphasizes a local focus,

> The Moscow branch of the foundation has been operating since August 2014. The trustees of the Amazing Fund each month form a grant of 30,000 rubles and invest it in a favorite project. The Fund considers any projects from any sphere: science, art, business, social projects.
>
> We give preference to those projects that are:-feasible (grant should be a tangible support for the development of the project); -socially significant, useful; -Create something new; -and, of course, just amazing!

The financial contributions made by the Awesome Foundation are clearly identified as grants, they are clear in the organizational mandate that there are no strings attached "We do not wish for the funds to be repaid."

Defining awesome

So what exactly constitutes awesome? The foundation is fairly open to definitions of that term. As one website describes "Truthfully . . . we don't really know. That's partly what makes this Foundation so great. But there is some general criteria that we've come up with to help define it. For us, awesome ideas have all or some combination of the following qualities. They are:

1   Memorable
2   Random/unexpected/out of the norm
3   Positive or will yield positive outcomes
4   Unique or take a unique twist on something common
5   Smile-worthy (the idea makes many people smile)
6   Awesome for more than just you
7   Worthy of the statement 'Yes! That's awesome!' "

(http://awesomehalifax.com)

Although the motivations in both of these examples are quite different, as we look at the constitution of organizational identity in each case, there are some interesting similarities as well. From a CCO perspective, we can understand these comparisons by employing McPhee and Zaug's (2000) Four Flows approach. This framework, as delimitated in previous chapters, asserts that the presence of these four flows is a necessary condition in the constitution of organization (Putnam & McPhee, 2008).

The first of these flows, organization-membership negotiation, is key to the communicative structure in each case. This focus typically includes socialization, identification and self-positioning activities (McPhee & Iverson, 2009). The communication pieces developed around both crowdfunding initiatives were very much focused on socialization. At the eatery contributors are encouraged to socialize as they claim the rewards of their investment, and in the Awesome example, the community engagement part of the initiative is forefront in its promotion. The Awesome initiative, however, has a much looser definition of membership, and is open to anyone who wants to be involved, "no strings attached." The Battery Park project is an investment, and based on a financial transaction of value for money.

The second flow, reflexive self-structuring, reflects rules and procedures for organizing (Aten & Thomas, 2016, p. 152). Although these cases both purport to be radically different approaches, 'breaking the rules' to traditional business, they do have rules and procedures for business which reflect their particular motivations. These rules are further defined within the technology in which they exist. So for example, communication patterns, application processes, membership registration, etc., are structured based on the technological influence of the platform on which they occur. The third flow, organizational activity coordination, essentially defines the ways in which the core of the organization connects with its members. This flow looks quite different in the two examples.

Using the Netlytic social media analyzer to view these two networks, I pulled out the visual data reflecting nodes and edges. Nodes in this case typically represent individuals, organizational units or organizations, while edges commonly represent flows of communication or information, advice or influence, or goods or services (Brass, Galaskiewicz, Greve, & Tsai, 2004).

The nodes and edges of the social media network reflecting the Battery Park project indicate a very centralized communication pattern with information, for the most part, exchanging between the core organization out to its members, and then individual members responding to the core. There is little intra-member communication indicated, but a very high degree of centrality and responsiveness between the organization and individual members.

The Awesome Foundation network is much more diverse. The conversations happen in a very dispersed way between various chapters of the organization, and loosely between individuals involved in local projects. Although the identity of the organization on its Twitter platform, for example, clearly reflects its global status, there is little communication between chapters, or between chapters and with the parent organization.

The fourth communication flow as described by McPhee and Iverson (2009), is that of institutional positioning. This flow refers to the external communication, or the way in which the organization positions itself within a broader field. In both cases discussed previously, this is a challenging endeavor for the organization. The struggle to carve out distinct space within a congested social media environment is evident in the way both organizations spend energy highlighting their distinctiveness.

One element that is common to both examples here as they relate to positioning is the way in which the organizations move between virtual and physical space in their efforts to engage their networks. One of the cautions around virtual organizing is the reliance on social media understandings of engagement, which may not translate into real-world actions. In both these cases, the translation of engagement into action in real space, i.e. eating in a restaurant or constructing a community-based project, challenge our understanding of engagement to include actions occurring in public space, offline.

Gerbaudo (2012) advocates for a broader understanding of social media space to go beyond the virtual or visual world. His works discuss the implications of moving between the virtual and the physical world through what he describes as a "choreography of assembly" understood as a process of symbolic construction of public space, which revolves around an emotional 'scene-setting' and 'scripting' (Alexander et al., 2006, p. 36) of participants' physical assembling. This translates into the construction of new forms of face-to-face organizing, i.e. directing individuals to public spaces, and creating new forms of proximity.

In the following chapters we will look at some variations on collective organizing through social media to further expand the discussion of the Four Flows approach to our understanding of virtual organizing.

7 Plausibility and legitimation

By analyzing intersections of plausibility and legitimation, we are able to see points of connection in the sensemaking process whereby the property of plausibility is strengthened in relation to other properties with the introduction of various legitimation strategies. This chapter will focus on the relationship between plausibility and legitimation strategies and practices within the social media environment as they relate to organizational identity.

Within a social media context, I am particularly interested in the intersection of these two elements: the sensemaking property of plausibility, a property influencing sensemaking as one meaning emerges as 'feeling right' or resonating above others, and discursive legitimacy, the privileging of one narrative or sense of an identity surfaces above others in a contested communicative environment. Individuals and organizations, remember, are striving for a plausible meaning in their efforts to normalize a changing or volatile situation. Following a shock, "efforts are made to construct a plausible sense of what is happening, and this sense of plausibility normalizes the breach, restores the expectation, and enable projects to continue" Weick and Sutcliffe (as cited in Navis & Glynn, 2011, p. 488).

Despite his work on faulty decisions that have resulted from plausible versus accurate sensemaking, Weick (2010) emphasizes the power of this property to influence other forms of sensemaking in the absence of strong alternatives. He also reminds us that plausible meanings

> tap into an ongoing sense of current climate, are consistent with other data, facilitate ongoing projects, reduce equivocality, provide an aura of accuracy (e.g. reflect the views of a consultant with a strong track record), and offer a potentially exciting future.
>
> (Weick et al., 2005, p. 415)

The intersection between plausibility and sensemaking is a clear one, they produce and maintain each other. Legitimacy is an important ingredient in the constitution of plausibility, and as Navis and Glynn explain, "plausibility ensues with the surety of legitimacy" (2011, p. 489).

Munro and Huber (2012), in their study of the limits of sensemaking, contrast Weick's use of plausibility as a way to explain failed sensemaking, with Kafka's view of plausibility as "a means of drawing us ever deeper into the labyrinthine folds of an indecipherable social order" (Munro & Huber, 2012, p. 536). From both these perspectives, there is an acknowledgment that plausibility occurs through a complex process of weaving understandings of how the world works, with understandings of how the organization works, and weighing these against personal experiences and expectations. It is a process which draws meaning from multiple sources.

Thus, the process of sensemaking is ultimately and fundamentally about "the ongoing development of plausible images that rationalize what people are doing" (Patriotta & Brown, 2011, p. 35). Sensemaking has further been described as a "search for plausibility and coherence, that is reasonable and memorable, which embodies past experience and expectations, and maintains the self while resonating with others" (Brown et al., 2008, p. 1038).

This description of an ongoing process to surface plausible meaning draws on many influences. The literature on discursive forms of legitimation tackles a number of these perspectives, looking at the different rhetorical practices which create a narrative, or an alternative explanation as legitimate, authentic and plausible.

Vaara and Tienari (2008, p. 988), for example, draw on the work of van Leeuwen and Wodak (1999), to present five categories of legitimation strategy: normalization, authorization, rationalization, moralization and narrativization. Normalization is described as a form of authorization whereby events or actions are constructed as normal or natural; authorization refers to legitimation related to the authority of laws, customs or individuals who hold some type of institutional authority; rationalization references actions based upon specific knowledge claims that are accepted as relevant or 'true' in a given context; moralization strategies are constructed by referencing specific value systems; and narrativization refers to the processes of situating the action within a relevant or accepted storytelling framework.

These discursive approaches "allow a shift in focus from established senses of legitimacy to ongoing discursive struggles for legitimation and, thus, increase our understanding of the micro level political dynamics of these processes" (Vaara & Tienari, 2008, p. 987). Through the enactment of these different strategies, organizational members craft narratives which compete to establish the plausibility, or authenticity of one particular understanding over another.

Legitimation within a social media network draws on these same rhetorical strategies, to some extent, but there are other tangible elements that contribute to the construction of the narrative. The edges and nodes within the network are visible markers of the size and scope of the network, and the potential distribution of the identity. There are also quantifiable records of the ways in which communication has transferred across the network through tweets, posts, likes, shares and re-tweets, for example. These artifacts of the network serve to further legitimate some narratives over others as evidence of 'likes' emerges. Through a CSM lens, these elements may serve to further constrain the range of possible narratives which retain their plausibility over time.

In contrast, however, social media also open channels of communication which offer conflicting interests, counter-discourses and even dissenting voices (Schultz, Castello, & Morsing, 2013). This multivocal context in which narratives emerge can further challenge existing legitimation processes. Yet, as Glozer, Caruana, and Hibbert (2018) emphasize,

> we still know relatively little about the micro-level processes of legitimation in these 'e-democratic' (Barros, 2014) and 'persistent' (Boyd, 2014; Treem & Leonardi, 2013) communicative contexts and, more poignantly, how these processes contribute to a new understanding of legitimation in fluid, open-ended and 'live' communication contexts (Kaplan & Haenlein, 2010).
>
> (p. 11)

According to Glozer et al. (2018), discursive legitimation in social media can be understood as a competitive process between contested positions and counter interests. This 'struggle' between contradictory interests for legitimation (Suddaby & Greenwood, 2005; Zilber, 2007) can be seen in this context as discursive process to constrain the range of voices within the formative context in which the communication occurs. Ultimately, this strategy would serve to remove dissenting voices (Ashforth & Gibbs, 1990) and thereby increase the legitimacy of the remaining narrative. Previous work on legitimation has characterized this construct as "organizational conformity to a socially constructed set of norms, values, beliefs and definitions" (Suchman, 1995; Glozer et al., 2018, p. 11). However, more recent work has expanded this understanding of legitimacy to acknowledge a processual approach, where legitimacy is constructed through social processes among multiple actors (Suddaby et al., 2017). This broader conceptualization has led to increased attention on the social processes through which legitimacy is "established as a communicative process of legitimation (Dowling, MacDonald, & Protter, 1983; Lammers, 2011; Patriotta, Gond, & Schultz, 2011; Suddaby, 2011)" (Glozer et al., 2018, p. 4).

Glozer et al. (2018) further explain that the potential of social media to facilitate social processes of legitimation, while creating spaces for otherwise marginalized voices, is found not just in the sheer number of voices that are able to access and participate in the conversation, but in the performative relationships these individuals have with both the production and consumption of content. Social media technologies, therefore, arguably expand the polyphonic setting, not just in allowing a greater number of individuals to participate, but by affording accessibility and continuity of dialogue across temporal boundaries (e.g. social media archives) and greater relational and content ties across online 'spaces' (e.g. 'liking' to content) (Treem & Leonardi, 2013). They transform knowledge sharing 'from an intermittent, centralised knowledge management process to a continuous online knowledge conversation of strangers, unexpected interpretations and re-uses, and dynamic emergence' (Majchrzak, Faraj, Kane, & Azad, 2013, p. 38). Such insights are particularly telling given the ostensibly performative nature of these organisational 'texts' in constructing organisational identity and legitimacy (Albu & Etter, 2016; Blaschke et al., 2012).

(Glozer et al., 2018, p. 8)

In their study of the legitimation strategies employed in online environments, Glozer et al. (2018) identified three forms of legitimation which occur in social media: discursive authorizing, discursive validation and discursive finalization. Discursive authorizing is described as a process of building personal and mythic credibility, contributing to legitimation processes through the establishment of voice in "polyphonic social media dialogue" (p. 18). The second process of legitimation, discursive validation, is described as a way of bolstering or strengthening the position of a particular narrative within a social media discussion through emphasizing moral arguments about 'the right thing to do' or revealing logical inconsistencies between organizational rhetoric and actions. The third process, discursive finalization, illustrates rhetorical strategies whereby efforts to draw dialogues toward an outcome, in some cases by antagonism or cooptation, are employed.

In particular, the processes of discursive authorizing and discursive validation resonate most closely with the intersection of plausibility and legitimation in social media from a sensemaking perspective. As organizations work to influence sensemaking properties within the constraints of an extant formative context, their discursive strategies within new media must conform to the range to possibilities available within established parameters. In that sense, the normative processes which are produced by and productive of societal-level discourses such as capitalism, globalization, nationalism, etc., serve to constrain the potential of social media to be e-democratic, or revolutionary. Although these media may serve to communicatively construct resistance, this exists only within the same spectrum as the power being enforced. As a result, social media function within the exertion of power from both the normative and dominant power discourses which impose order on society, and the potential of technological vehicles that offer that 'polyphonic' (multi-vocal) social media settings might "pluralise discourses that construct legitimacy" (Etter, Colleoni, Illia, Meggiorin, & D'Eugenio, 2017, p. 11).

Formative context

Critical Sensemaking incorporates the properties of sensemaking. I have focused on plausibility and identity construction in this chapter, but also the rules within which these operate and the formative context that enfolds the process, ultimately defining the range of possibilities which are available to individual sensemakers. This formative context refers to what Roberto Unger (1987) describes as a combination of institutional and imaginative arrangements that serve to maintain and obfuscate underlying tensions and conflicts. These arrangements are what underpin social organization, and ultimately constitute a stabilizing force in which social struggles are played out and constrained (Grant & Mills, 2006). Or as Blackler (1992, p. 279) describes it, "the imaginative schemas of participants interact with the institutional frameworks in which they operate."

This context is particularly important in discussing the property of plausibility, specifically, plausibility versus accuracy, as a determinant of which narratives will be taken up and which will not. As discussed in Chapter 2, the propensity of one narrative to dominate over a range of alternatives can result from a complex set of circumstances. The previous discussion regarding social process of legitimation concludes that the digital media environment is both transparent and constrained through rhetorical and discursive processes. However, it is important to point out that the technological structures employed in these networks are also included in this formative context. As Vallee (1982) asserts, in the very early work on public relations and technology, "Real power resides with those who set up the structure for others to think about because they define what is available, and what is not, what is recorded and what is forgotten" (p. 87).

Although scholarship on social media is now the fastest growing area of public relations research (Kent & Taylor, 2014), there has been very little critical analysis of the formative context in which these technologies exist. From that perspective, research on social media within this discipline requires in the long term a broader and deeper understanding of the ways in which the technological structures of social media both produce and constrain the legitimation of plausible narratives of identity. Kent and Taylor (2014) also articulate a caution about the potential of these technologies, and suggest that a healthy skepticism of social media technology may be warranted as we move toward future communication alternatives. They remind us of issues of privacy, for example, as well as authenticity. As Oram (2009, para. 22) states,

> this leads to the ultimate dilemma in Internet identity. The artificiality of our participation online, and the limited scope of available media, suggest that the Internet will never let us show our true selves. But other characteristics – the persistence of information and the ease of recombining information from different places – suggests just the opposite: that we can't conceal our true selves for long.

Kent and Taylor (2014) provide a further analysis of some of the themes which emerged in a 2014 study by Kent and Saffer (2014). One of those themes identified by 14 influential technology professionals and academics in a Delphi process was that of fragmentation. Expert participants indicated that fragmentation, not integration, would characterize the internet and society going forward. Kent and Taylor point out that research has emerged indicating that the potential of connectivity that was so embraced as the promise of the internet age has not been realized. Individuals are connected in growing numbers via social media technology, but only tenuously.

Those connections, which were originally understood as expanding an individual's range of possibilities in terms of plausible meanings, actually serve to narrow and then reinforce the limited number of plausible meanings from which the individual may choose. For example, Rainie and Smith (2012) found that almost 20% of social media users in their study had blocked, unfriended or hidden someone because that person posted something with which they did not agree or that person argued with them about a political or social point of view.

In addition to individual actions to remove dissent from the formative context, there are also structural elements of the technology, limiting the range of possible meanings to which social media users are exposed. This reflects a concern within the public relations literature about the growing personalization of constructed realities as algorithms increasingly determine the information which network members receive. Just and Latzer (2017) emphasize that "altogether, compared to reality construction by traditional mass media, algorithmic reality construction tends to increase individualization, commercialization, inequalities, and deterritorialization and to decrease transparency, controllability, and predictability" (p. 238).

Ultimately, the potential of a broadened, polyvonic, accessible formative context in which to make sense of the world is challenged by a convergence of structures, technological and social, and processes vying for legitimation in the digital landscape. What were previously barriers to sensemaking related to access to the conversation, technology to engage in the conversation and ability to communicate to a broad social audience, have largely been resolved by social media technologies. At the same time, the discursive constraints around processes of legitimation and the struggle to construct plausible meanings in a cluttered communication landscape result in the privileging of those narratives which are successful in asserting authority or imposing order.

Order and disorder

Weick has identified the purpose of sensemaking as a process of imposing order on chaos, or ordering the 'way things are done' back into an accepted routine. As previously discussed in Chapter 5, the premise behind the human propensity toward sensemaking is the need to resolve disorder brought on by a shock.

a vocabulary of sensemaking might start with these basics:

> Disorder + confusion + insecurity = trouble.
> Trouble + thinking = sensemaking.
> Probing for plausible stories that explain trouble = enacted sensemaking.
>
> (Weick, 2010, p. 543)

Both CSM and CCO frameworks start with a common assumption that communication organizes and "creates order out of potential disorder" (Cooren et al., 2011, p. 23). Even more, that assumption extends to suggest the processes of sensemaking and communication ultimately result in the constitution of organization. As Taylor and Van Every (2000, pp. 33–34) describe, "a situation is talked into being through the interactive exchanges of organizational members to produce a view of circumstances including the people, their objects, their institutions and history, and their siting [i.e. location as a site] in a finite time and place." As situations are talked into existence, a collective order is restored and sensemaking returns to routine business.

However, Cooren et al. (2011) assert that we may actually have much to learn from the study of disordering, along with the restoration of order.

> Longstanding beliefs about the functions of communication are that it is essential in solving important social problems, particularly those related to a perceived lack of community, a threat to cultural continuity, or a need for a smoothly-functioning social system (Pinchevski, 2005). The concern for order has a long sociological heritage, but some assert that disorganization and disordering should play a more central role in our conceptions of scholarship.
>
> (p. 23)

For example, Putnam et al. (2009, p. x) assert that CCO theory tends to center on the processes of communication that "produce patterns that endure over time and ones that constitute the organization as a whole" (x). However, they point out, Taylor (2009) advocate that the presence of communication produces organization, as long as organization meansgetting organized. They also agree that communication can ultimately disconnect as well as connect,

> disassemble as well as assemble. . . . The irony of communication is that it can separate at the same time that it connects. Even in the midst of 'ineffective and inefficient interaction,' organizing still occurs. Moreover, from a CCO view, what constitutes order or disorder is not always readily apparent. For example, a parent might view a teenage son's room as disorderly, but the appearance of disarray in the room might foster effective coordinated action and task accomplishment for the son.

In effect, CCO views would treat organizing and being organized as different constructs, both of them open to investigation.

(Putnam et al., 2010, p. 160)

Similar questions arise when considering the relative position of social media networks to organizations. Networks across social media platforms are always, arguably, in a state of becoming. If we draw on the Four Flows approach to CCO, membership negotiation in a network is an ongoing and important element in the establishment of what that 'organization' looks like. The process of 'friending,' or 'blocking' someone into or out of a network reflects an ongoing negotiation, while the network itself continues on in a constant state of flux. This disorder offer both diversity and challenge as members collectively work to maintain routines.

Organizational crisis is another area where disorder, which we may see also as shocks to sensemaking, becomes evident. From a public relations perspective, crisis communication is one of the most challenging areas of organizational identity construction. Over the past two decades social media have both facilitated crises and helped to resolve them through the communicative work to reconstitute organization during and after a crisis. An organizational crisis here is defined as "a low-probability, high-impact event that threatens the viability of the organization and is characterized by ambiguity of cause, effect, and means of resolution, as well as by a belief that decisions must be made swiftly" (Pearson & Clair, 1998, p. 60).

Research has consistently shown that organizational crises result in increased activity on social media networks. Perry, Taylor, and Doerfel (2003) found that organizations increased their own usage of social media during times of crisis, most notably for the purposes of engaging stakeholders, facilitating two-way interactions with their networks, and providing crisis-related updates. In 2005 Taylor and Perry identified innovative media tactics being utilized by organizations in crises, pointing to dialogic communication, connecting links, real-time monitoring, multimedia effects and online chat lines. They also found organizations were using the internet and particularly social media platforms to circumvent the gatekeeping function of mainstream media and tell their side of the story (Coombs & Holladay, 2008).

Likewise, Weick (1988) reminds us that organizational crises are sites of increased sensemaking, as they are points in the organization's history where routines are disrupted. In his foundational work in this area, 'Enacted Sensemaking in Crisis Situations,' Weick challenged communication scholars to reflect on what had widely been thought of as crises related to technological or logistical failures in a different light. His contention was that the human element of sensemaking, or more accurately failed sensemaking, was actually the key component of the crises.

In their review of work on crisis and sensemaking, Maitlis et al. (2010) categorize the extant literature in two ways. The first is a body of research on how sensemaking unfolds during crisis, and the second is a body of work which looks at how sense is made of crises after they happen. In the first case, research includes

> mining disasters (Wicks, 2002), climbing disasters (Kayes, 2004), and disasters in entertainment events (Vendelo & Rerup, 2009), as well as Weick's work on the Bhopal accident (Weick, 2010), the Tenerife air crash (Weick, 1990) and the Mann Gulch fire (Weick, 1993).
>
> (Maitlis et al., 2010, p. 554)

The second area of research, reflecting on sensemaking after crises happen, tended to draw on public inquiries, reports and documents that have constructed accounts of the events. These include work by Brown (2000); Shiravastava, Mitroff, Miller, and Miclani (1988); and Turner (1976). These studies focus on events which were seen as "micro-level sensemaking practices produce the macro social order" (Maitlis et al., 2010, p. 555).

Findings from this study highlighted some important themes. First, "individual's early, positive, public evaluations shape sensemaking in crisis preventing them and others from bracketing contradictory cues until it is much too late (Salancik & Pfeffer, 1978; Weick & Sutcliffe, 2003)" (p. 555).

In Weick et al. (2005, p. 411) the process of noticing and bracketing is described as "an incipient state of sensemaking." In this context sensemaking means basically "inventing a new meaning (interpretation) for something that has already occurred during the organizing process, but does not yet have a name (italics in original), has never been recognized as a separate autonomous process, object, event" (Magala, 1997, p. 324 as cited in Weick et al., 2005, p. 410).

Weick et al. (2005, p. 412) continue that

> the more general point is that in the early stages of sensemaking, phenomena 'have to be forcibly carved out of the undifferentiated flux of raw experience and conceptually fixed and labeled so that they can become the common currency for communicational exchanges' (Chia, 2000, p. 517). Notice that once bracketing occurs, the world is simplified.

In times of crisis, bracketing may occur to differentiate between pre and post crisis, for example, as individuals struggle to establish a frame wherein the new context or unfamiliar events are connected to previously familiar experiences. During a crisis, bracketing may follow an event, but the labeling process – where an event or series of events becomes a crisis – follows. "A mistake follows an act. It identifies the character of an act in its aftermath. It names it. An act, however, is not mistaken; it becomes mistaken" (Paget, 1988, p. 56). Weick et al. (2005) further explain that when a mistake is bracketed, the event itself is in an advanced stage, and the labeling is retrospective. We can apply this description to organizational crisis in the same way, understanding that the process of bracketing and labeling a crisis is directed in great part by the retrospective nature of sensemaking, and the sensemaker's past experiences.

And secondly, the Maitlis et al. (2010) study showed that sensemaking "in a crisis is cumulatively influenced by the institutional contexts in which the organization and its members are embedded, and that sensemaking about crises often serves to maintain these institutions" (p. 555).

This point in particular emphasizes the importance of the formative context, enacted through organizational rules and discursive practices. As discussed in Chapter 3, the formative context sets up the range of possible alternatives within the sensemaking process, establishing the plausibility of some narratives over others. As described in the work of Maitlis referenced earlier, the tendency of sensemaking is to reinforce existing support for the institutions which frame the organization's previous experience.

Social media networks and technologies in particular facilitate this process, as they offer immediate and accessible opportunities for shared reflection. In their research on one specific social media platform, Heverin and Zach (2012) investigated the role of micro-blogging during crises and established that micro-blogging provided a useful forum for collective sensemaking as the crises unfolded. During the initial stages of the crises, this platform was used mainly for information sharing about the events unfolding. Over time, however, the communication centered more so on the collective sensemaking occurring as organizational and community members attempted to make sense of the crises.

Human and non-human actants

Another element of the sensemaking process which works to simplify and restore order to a chaotic environment is the relationship between human and non-human elements in the organization. The nature of organizations from a CCO perspective is precarious and subject to change as they are continuously constituted and re-constituted within a changing communication environment. As described by Schoeneborn and Trittin (2013, p. 193) "organizations are stabilized by various non-human entities." The CCO perspective suggests that organizations, and the sensemaking that occurs within them, are stabilized to some extent by the presence of these entities in the form of texts, scripts or routines which 'act' on the organization's behalf (Cooren et al., 2011; Schoeneborn &Trittin, 2013). These phenomenon are interpreted quite broadly, and may include tangible elements such as text or intangibles such as informal practices or ideas about the way things are done.

In his work using Critical Sensemaking, Hartt (2013) introduced synergies between that framework and Actor Network Theory to identify the 'non-corporeal actant' present in sensemaking and organizing. In Hartt's work a "sub group of actants termed non-corporeal actants is coined. This group refers to reified values, beliefs, concepts, and ideas which have no physical entity (corpus) but interact with the other human or non- human actors/actants of the network" (p. 19).

This concept of the non-corporeal actant broadens the category of non-human entities that serve to stabilize organization. Not only can this grouping include text, routine and scripts, we can also include organizational rules and social discourse which inform the formative context in which the organization exists. And in a social media context, this grouping of elements is even more interesting as what were previously abstract; i.e. conversations, thoughts and localized communication now may become globally accessible and durable as they are shared along social networks.

Here we return to the question of agency within organization, as the CCO-CSM framework begins to identify sites of agency with processes of organization, identity and sensemaking. The Foucauldian perspective of power and agency which informs our understanding of the power-knowledge relationship suggests that agency is subject to constraint from the power effects of discourse. Likewise, as this power dynamic functions in the formative context of organizational sensemaking, alternative narratives or meanings may be de-legitimized, or privileged, in relation to others. This impacts the plausibility of a particular meaning, and therefore the sensemaking available to individuals.

Referring again to Actor Network Theory, Putnam et al. (2010, p. 163) suggest the notion of inscription to clarify the role of non-human actants in the form of text:

> that is, the material and structural exist as texts, such as documents and policies reified from past interactions, and as material objects, such as buildings and furniture, that impose on and are shaped by organizing processes. Organizations as entities, then, also function as inscriptions of materiality. Thus, CCO research that centers on communicative aspects of inscriptions is one approach to materiality. An alternative approach is to investigate the role of objects, sites, and bodies, not primarily in terms of how communication generates organizing but as an outgrowth or consequence of the meeting of material and ideational worlds (Ashcraft et al., 2009).

The work of Cooren (2004) tackles the question of agency among non-human actants in organizations. He suggests that individual texts, or non-human entities, have agency once they leave the hands of the speaker, or writer, or in the case of social media, perhaps texter. In the case of social media, text clearly takes on an agency of its own depending upon how it is shared or liked, and contextualized within and beyond the network. As an item 'goes viral,' it becomes a durable artifact of the network/organization and begins to call others into action.

In the case of an organizational crisis, where identity is challenged, or a shock occurs in organizational sensemaking, the non-human entities which circulate within the network as social media posts and other forms of content take on agency and call others into action as the crisis is made sense of from different stakeholder perspectives.

Understanding these elements – abstract, non-human, etc. – as constituting organization and facilitating both order and disorder, is a necessary shift in both public relations scholarship and practice. This requirement is highlighted most notably in the context of social media technologies. As Kent (2013, p. 344) points out,

> Most of the social media technologies that were supposed to connect people to others, stimulate our democracy, and enable every citizen to participate in the life of the mind, have largely had just the opposite effect. As public communicators, we control perhaps the most important resource in a democracy: information. To date, our lack of understanding of new technology, and implementation of new technologies simply to serve marketing and advertising interests have led to less civic participation, and less awareness of what is happening in the world around us. Indeed, for more than three decades, scholars have argued that new technologies have negative as well as positive aspects, but we have mostly ignored the negatives.

See, for examples, the work of (Burnham, 1984; Kent, 2008; Postman, 1993; Taylor & Kent, 2010).

That is to say, communicative processes of sensemaking and organization are not simply tools to be applied in the pursuit of specific organizational ends such as marketing initiatives or reputation management. They are collective processes which create meaning, establish order (and disorder) and define the range of possibilities for sensemaking alternatives.

8 Volkswagen – truth, accuracy and plausibility

The previous two chapters covered some of the issues and opportunities related to processes of legitimation and the struggle to establish plausibility within a digital media context. The impetus for organizations to construct plausible narratives of identity is never more urgently felt than during times of organizational crisis. In this chapter I will discuss the organizational identity of Volkswagen, specifically during the 2015–2016 emissions control scandal. During this period, it was discovered Volkswagen had developed and installed emissions control system software or 'defeat devices' in model year 2009–2015 vehicles with 2.0 liter diesel engines. The company admitted it had installed the software, and much of the fallout was documented or debated across social media. This was a high-profile scandal, and it continues two years later as special hearings, vehicle buy-backs, and other organizational strategies roll out. Social media platforms in this case, and more generally, have transformed the way we see organizational crises unfold, offering both increased access to information and accessible opportunities for individuals to voice their opinions and concerns. For this analysis, I offer a deconstruction of textual data gathered through Twitter.

Background

In 2015, the US Environmental Protection Agency (EPA), revealed that the Volkswagen Group (VW Group) had produced cars that contained software to manipulate emissions tests. This software, termed a 'defeat device' meant the vehicles could detect when they were being tested and alter their natural behavior. Essentially that meant that the affected VW Group vehicles would produce far less pollutants when under test conditions than when on the road being used by ordinary people day to day. The pollutants which were produced were NOx emissions, which are particularly harmful to human health. Volkswagen admitted that about 11 million cars worldwide were fitted with the devices (Hotten, 2015).

This revelation was troubling to Volkswagen customers and others for many reasons, but the two primary concerns expressed through public outrage during the scandal were corporate corruption and environmental damage. These were both damaging to the VW organizational identity, perhaps the environmental element more so, as the corporate brand had been for years reflecting an environmentally friendly organization.

Social media were immediately engaged in sharing this information, and Twitter was at the forefront of the communication. One of the first tweets to break the news was posted at 8:49 a.m.

PDT by @davidshepardson, Detroit News DC Bureau Chief.
David Shepardson Verified account @davidshepardson
Breaking: @EPA announcing major enforcement against @VW, @detroit news has learned. 8:49 AM – 18 Sep 2015 from Washington, DC

Social media reaction to the scandal was swift. On Monday, the 21st of September, the Twitter conversation on this topic reached an impressive peak of more than 80,000 daily tweets. Over the following week more than 1.3 million tweets were posted by users all over the world, and on average, more than 8,000 tweets were posted per hour about Volkswagen (Parker, 2015).

On Twitter, rhetorical strategies were quickly enacted on both sides of the story in this case, with the Volkswagen organization performing strategies of attribution in the pursuit of plausible explanations and image management. At the same time, customers and other stakeholders enacted a process of resistance through construction of an online identity around the hashtag #dieselgate. Other related hashtags emerged #VWscandal, etc.

#dieselgate

On the same day that the crisis broke, a dedicated hashtag emerged on Twitter, #dieselgate. It appeared for the first time on September 18th:

Drew Smith @drewpasmith

In light of #dieselgate I'm more convinced than ever that a 6-litre V12 is the way forward.
11:59 AM – 18 Sep 2015 from Tottenham, London

@drewpasmith der 1. Erwähnung der #dieselgate erscheint auf Ihrer TL. Jetzt ist Trending Topic in Deutschland! #trndnl

(Mention of #dieselgate appears in your tweet. Now it is a trending topic in Germany! #trndnl)

The hashtag appeared in a limited way over that weekend, but by the following Monday, it had been used 948 times, and by the end of the week, it had appeared in 39,295 tweets.

The nodes and edges within this network indicated that by the end of the six-week period following the EPA announcement high-profile media accounts (both on Twitter and in mainstream media) were using the #dieselgate hashtag, and in many languages (Parker, 2015). This trans-media dissemination of the hashtag ultimately helped the crisis to become a world-wide trending topic on Twitter.

The dedicated hashtag and a constrained range of possibilities in the conversation

When Twitter's developers launched the platform in March 2006, the purpose of the technology was somewhat unclear. The debate was around whether it would serve as a technology providing updates, from person to person, or as a mechanism to facilitate conversations among many people. The structural limitations of the first iteration of Twitter meant that it was the former, a method of sending updates and to target a recipient one would use the @ sign to signify a 'handle' and thereby identify a specific recipient who would track your updates.

The following year, Chris Messina, an early Twitter user, suggested using hashtags by adopting the Internet Relay Chat (IRC) convention, which resulted in the Twitter tagging feature, hashtags. Now the hashtag, a series of words or phrase prefixes with a pound sign # is the main way in which Twitter users organize and communicate. The introduction of the hashtag also allowed for a 'trending' feature to emerge. In these cases, the most popular hashtags being used on the platform at a particular time are highlighted in a side navigation bar as trending (Chang, 2010).

Crisis communication

An organizational crisis is the "perception of an unpredictable event that threatens important expectancies of stakeholders and can seriously impact an organization's performance and generate negative outcomes" (Coombs, 2007, pp. 2–3). In this case, although the predictability of the crisis may be debatable, the EPA revelation and ensuing social media storm resulted in serious negative outcomes for Volkswagen. By December 2015 sales of VW vehicles had dropped by 20% (Painter & Martins, 2017).

That negativity was not reflected everywhere, the Guardian reported on October 20, 2015 that a German poll showed two-thirds of respondents still trusted the VW brand, felt the scandal had been exaggerated, and expected the whole thing to be forgotten within a year (Lohr, 2015).

Crisis communication strategies in this case can be understood as both CCO approaches and examples of CSM process reflecting plausibility, identity construction and the boundaries of rules and discourse operating at both the organizational and societal level.

Influencers and context

As events unfolded, tweets increased or decreased in direct response to what was happening in the mainstream media or through other events. Similar reviews of the Twitter activity surrounding this crisis support this assessment (i.e. Stieglitx, Mirbabaie, & Potthoff, 2018) suggesting that real-life incidents trigger social media communication.

This indicates that activity of the mainstream news media, and the "real-world" events surrounding this crisis trigger the need for social media users to communicate on platforms like Twitter (Stieglitz et al., 2018, p. 519). This process unfolded visually as I analyzed networked communication as shocks, in this case representing a series of revelations and events which occurred in rapid succession, triggering sensemaking within social media communities.

From a CSM perspective, this relationship between online and offline experience is interesting. Clearly, events and experience which happen offline can provide the shocks which trigger sensemaking enacted in the online world, and vice versa. This point is perhaps most clearly made by the impact of social media conversation on VW stock price during these early days of the scandal. During this first week, Volkswagen's stock price dropped from a high of $169 to a low of $95. As the tweets increased, the stock price decreased (unionmetrics.com).

Analysis of text and context

In my analysis of the Twitter data available during the first six weeks of the scandal, I reviewed content, handles and hashtags, as well as mention of events which could constitute shocks in the sensemaking environment, i.e. hearings, speeches, recalls, etc. Content was coded for sensemaking processes, alternating between the individual tweets emerging and the context within which the data produced a textual whole. This approach allowed for continued questioning of findings as indicated in my signposts as outlined in Chapter 4. As described there, I employed an abductive approach reflecting both the application of deductive codes identified in the sensemaking process, and an awareness of the role of the researcher in the production of the meanings which are surfaced and the context in which they are understood.

The first challenge to making sense of the Twitter data in this case was the volume of tweets which occurred within a very short timeframe.

Before this news broke, there were on average 10,000 tweets posted every day about Volkswagen. That number jumped to more than 100,000 daily tweets during the peak of the crisis in late September. There were more than 53,000 tweets about Volkswagen on September 18. In the two days between that Friday and the following Monday the Twitter conversation was relatively contained. However, on September 21 conversations about the scandal began trending (unionmetrics.com).

I tracked tweets from the date the scandal broke, September 18, 2015, for a six-week period, until the end of October 2015. I limited my tracking to tweets that used the keywords 'Dieselgate' 'Volkswagen,' 'VW,' 'emission scandal' or the handle @VW and @Volkswagen – the two main global

Volkswagen corporate accounts. Tweets were limited to English tweets, and the content of the retrieved tweets had to be related to the scandal. In total I analyzed just over 300,000 tweets in this period.

The tone and content of these Tweets reflected findings from other social media studies (i.e. Merli, 2015), and confirmed, not surprisingly, that the majority of messages were 'very negative' and addressed concerns about the organization's reputation, trustworthiness and commitment to the environment. Approximately one quarter of the tweets reviewed discussed the quality of the vehicles produced. In contrast another 20% attempted to provide somewhat positive comments, defending the history of the brand and encouraging Volkswagen to 'do the right thing,' although it was not entirely clear, beyond accountability, what that would be.

Within the myriad of twitter conversations happening during this time, Volkswagen itself produced relatively few tweets during the crisis. These tweets reflected two sensemaking and, in essence, sense-giving processes aimed at constructing a plausible explanation for the discovery of the 'defeat devices.' As rhetorical strategies, Volkswagen's messaging essentially worked to attribute responsibility and reinforce corporate ethics.

Plausible attribution

This case study gets at the question of authentic identity in social media from another perspective. As the sensemaking around plausible explanations for the emissions defeat technology began, Volkswagen was quick to provide attribution or plausible alternatives to address both image management and establish voice in a multitude of social media messages expressing outrage.

These rhetorical strategies focus specifically on shifting blame for the deceit on to a 'group' or at least some small number of rogue engineers who had made some bad choices.

> Volkswagen's US CEO testified Thursday that the decision to use emissions cheating software was not made at the corporate level. Instead, it was 'software engineers who put this in for whatever reason,' Michael Horn told a congressional panel that is investigating the scandal.
>
> (Puzzanghera & Hirsch, 2015)

By analyzing the nodes (people) in the Twitter network as well as the edges (relationships) between the people in the network, we can begin to get an idea of who is talking to whom during the crisis. Interestingly in this case, the 'Chain' network, identifying who responds to whom in the network, indicates that Volkswagen did not engage in a sustained or visible two-way communication strategy. Information from the organization went out into the network, but the organization did not reply to other users, rarely responding to tweets either directed at them or in response to an organizational tweet.

The 'Name' network, or who mentions whom, in the Twitter conversation indicates that although there were a very large number of tweets generated during this period, the top ten users generated more than 2,000 tweets each. In essence, these very active users dominated certainly the volume of conversation occurring. Their role in extracting cues from a complex and rapidly unfolding environment made them important elements of the sensemaking process.

The data gathered from Twitter around the #dieselgate network indicated that nodes and edges are evident in a number of conversations which appear to be happening within several different groups. The nodes, or people, in the conversation are scattered across the network and do not reflect a centralized communication process. There is very little interaction with Volkswagen itself, aside from re-tweets and reaction to tweets, but very little engagement in terms of the flow of communication back and forth. The edges, connections, between these conversations indicate that the communication is dispersed, with the space functioning more as a forum for sharing comments than an opportunity for organization or interaction.

'Two rogue engineers'

Although Volkswagen didn't communicate frequently during the six-weeks' period after the charges were laid, the messages which did come from the organization focused on essentially two main ideas, the first is that this deception was perpetrated by two rogue engineers, as described by VW's US chief executive officer. This idea was repeated in further communication characterized as a 'few software engineers' or a 'handful of engineers' (Kravets, 2015), but the idea was clearly centered around a rogue group of employees and not the doing of the organization as a whole, certainly not organizational leadership. The second idea which permeated the Volkswagen discourse, online and offline, was that the corporation was still an ethical organization with ethical core principles. Most notably, the core principle of being environmentally friendly.

In this strategy of both attributing blame for the deception to a small number of rogue engineers (Painter & Martins, 2017) and reminding the public of a prior focus on environmental sustainability, Volkswagen attempted to influence the formative context in which sensemaking would happen around this crisis.

Another strategy of the Situational Crisis Communication Theory (Coombs & Holladay, 2010) approach appears in the tweets from Volkswagen in September and October, 2015, that of corporate apology.

Apology

During the search period, only 34 original tweets were identified as coming from the organization, Volkswagen or its national-level organizations.

Furthermore, 17 of those tweets did not contain scandal-related content. Within the remaining tweets, only two were specifically crafted as apologies. One of those was titled Update from Volkswagen regarding the EPA investigation, and the second was labeled Video statement of Prof. Dr. Martin Winterkorn. Neither of these texts clearly indicated an apology in the title, and the video statement required readers to click through to another link.

Volkswagen USA Verified account @VW

Update from Volkswagen regarding the EPA investigation:

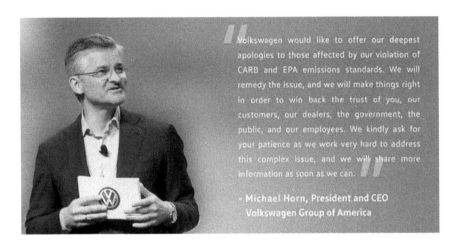

Volkswagen would like to offer our deepest apologies to those affected by our violation of CARB and EPA emissions standards. We will remedy the issue, and we will make things right in order to win back the trust of you, our customers, our dealers, the government, the public, and our employees. We kindly ask for your patience as we work very hard to address this complex issue, and we will share more information as soon as we can.

– Michael Horn, President and CEO
Volkswagen Group of America

8:27 PM – 24 Sep 2015

Volkswagen Verified account @Volkswagen

Video statement of Prof. Dr. Martin Winterkorn: www.volkswagen-media-services.com/en/detailpage/-/detail/Video-statement-Prof-Dr-Martin-Winterkorn-English/view/2718368/7a5bbec13158edd433c6630f5ac445da?p_p_auth=9iRucc6i . . .

4:33 PM – 22 Sep 2015

According to Coombs and Holladay (2010), the corporate apology should serve to alleviate some of the public anger or frustration around the crisis. However, sensemaking in this instance did not reflect that outcome. Responses to the two apology tweets were, for the most part, negative in tone.

9 Engagement and enactment

Sensemaking is evidenced in the property of enactment. In this chapter, I will discuss the nature of enactment from within the sensemaking framework, highlighting the ways that meaning and identity are constructed through the actions (including language and text) of the sensemakers themselves. This form of active sensemaking coincides with the propensity toward user engagement which characterizes social media platforms.

In the previous examples we looked at the ways in which online organizing is communicatively constitute and can cross boundaries into the offline world, thus re-defining physical public spaces. This process of enactment highlights not just the transferability of sensemaking through different contexts, but from a CCO perspective, the ways in which flows of communication can unfold simultaneously in different spaces. This chapter will focus on the enactment of meaning from a perspective of political and social engagement via social media, with a particular interest in the enactment of resistance to dominant narratives.

In his work providing reflections on #Occupy, Juris (2012) calls for a shift in our understanding from a 'logic of networking' (Juris, 2008), which supports a framework of communication and networking among collective actors, to a 'logic of aggregation,' which involves the "assembling of masses of individuals from diverse backgrounds within physical spaces" (p. 260). It is this translation of enactment to a physical gathering and a re-defining of public space existing both on and offline which will ultimately contribute to plausible narratives of e-democratic change. Flanagin, Stohl, & Bimber (2006, p. 32) characterize this move toward e-democracy (Barros, 2014) as a way to "reframe collective action as being constituted by a set of communication practices involving the crossing of boundaries from the private to the public realm."

Postill (2013) provides us with an empirical example of this process taking place as he reflects on his experience with the Indignados (or 15M) movement in Spain, part of the global anti-austerity movements mobilizing in 2011. In the early hours of May 16 something unexpected happened. A group of some 40 protesters decided to set camp at Madrid's main square, Puerta del Sol, instead of returning to their homes. One of them, a member of the hacker group Isaac Hacksimov, explained later: "All we did was a gesture that broke the collective mental block (quoted in Sanchez, 2011)" (in Postill, 2013, p. 54). Fearing that the authorities would evict them, they sent out calls for support via the internet. The first person to join them learned about their action on Twitter.

By the following day their numbers had swollen to 200 and by May 20 there were nearly 30,000 people at the square. This demographic explosion was mirrored online (see figures as follows). Other cities around Spain followed suit, and the 15M movement was now a global media event (Postill, 2013, p. 54).

This interrelationship between enactment in public spaces and enactment in virtual public spaces created an interesting and emergent space in which sensemaking could occur. As communicative processes around membership negotiation expanded beyond the geographic borders of Madrid, to include virtual support from other areas of Spain and farther, the legitimacy of the 15M identity became increasingly plausible and authentic. As previously discussed, the process of sensemaking is triggered by shocks in our routines. Shocks are ambiguous or uncertain events that disrupt our routines and force us to deal with them. In the preceding example, it was the physical aggregation of organizational members itself that produced a shock to sensemaking, resulting in an expanded and engaged enactment of organizing both online and off.

Collective action, as collective sensemaking, across social media is largely seen as one of the great possibilities of this digital environment. As a result, there is a growing literature around political and social organizing within marginalized groups. Kavada (2015) provides an overview of a scholarship around collective action and social mobilization through digital media. For example, in this work the literature ranges from studies on mediatization of social movements (Mattoni & Trere, 2014), transmedia organizing and the immigrant rights movement (Costanza-Chock, 2014), and new technologies and social movements (Earl, Hunt, Garrett, & Dal, 2014).

With the high-profile organizing against repressive regimes in Egypt in the past decade, there is much discussion about the transformation and empowerment of oppressed groups. Social media guru Clay Shirky summarizes this potential in the following description:

> As the communications landscape gets denser, more complex, and more participatory, the networked population is gaining greater access to information, more opportunities to engage in public speech, and an enhanced ability to undertake collective action. In the political arena, as the protests in Manila demonstrated, these increased freedoms can help loosely coordinated publics demand change.
>
> (Shirky, 2011, p. 29)

Loader and Mercea (2011) provide an historical view of the potential of social media. The first wave of enthusiasm for internet-based visions of digital democracy was largely predicated upon the desire to produce virtual public spheres (Loader, 1997; Tambini, Bryan, & Tsagarousianou, 1998; Blumler & Gurevitch, 2001). Their contention is that "democratic governance could be significantly improved through the open and equal deliberation between citizens, representatives and policy-makers, afforded by the new information and communication technologies. For cyberlibertarians, this could even be achieved without the need for governments (Barlow, 1996)" (Loader & Mercea, 2011, p. 757).

Potential notwithstanding, as we have discussed in previous chapters, the range of possibilities available to sensemakers, individually and collectively, is constrained in various ways. To accept that because the technology is available e-democracy will follow is perhaps naive, given the variety of examples available to the opposite. As Gerbaudo (2012, p. 16) states,

> if Shirky is king of the techno-optimists, Belarusan scholar Evgenyi Morozov is the prince of techno-pessimists. Morozov, who had himself initially contributed to the celebratory discourse on social media, has more recently vigorously denounced the risks of 'slacktivism,' or activism for slackers. For Morozov slacktivisim is 'feel good activism that has zero political or social impact' but creates 'an illusion of having a meaningful impact on the world without demanding anything more than joining a Facebook group' (Morozov, 2009).

Slacktivism (a combination of the words activism and slacker) is defined by UrbanDictionary.com, as:

> The act of participating in obviously pointless activities as an expedient alternative to actually expending effort to fix a problem. Signing an email petition to stop rampant crime is slacktivism. Want to really make your community safer? Get off your ass and start a neighborhood watch!

This term was made popular in part by Malcolm Gladwell in the New Yorker (Gladwell, 2010) where he offered a harsh comparison between on-the-ground revolutions and social media activism which he saw as essentially low-risk and low-impact. An early example of this was highlighted as the large online support for the Save Darfur Facebook campaign in 2010, which did not translate into a corresponding level of meaningful offline action toward this cause. In fact, an estimated 98% of Facebook followers of this group did not donate financially to the cause at all (Corrigan, 2016).

Evidence such as the Darfour Campaign has contributed to the debate surrounding the role of social media in protest movements. Although there is agreement on the capacity of social media to rapidly amass audiences and mobilize them around particular issues, scholars contend that this type of collective action requires "only ephemeral engagements from participants" (Earl, Hunt, Garrett, & Dal, 2015, p. 1).

Dean (2012) points to the challenges inherent in this contradiction, highlighting that "[c]ommunication technologies contribute to the displacement and dispersion of critical energy such that even as inequality has intensified, forming and organizing a coherent opposition has remained a persistent problem." However, Shirky (2011) takes issue with the slacktivism argument asserting that, "The critique is correct but not central to the social media's power; the fact that barely committed actors cannot click their way to a better world does not mean that committed actors cannot use social media effectively" (p. 38)

If we can agree that there is potential for social movements to organize digitally and go on to transcend boundaries into physical, public spaces, how are these evolving organizations communicatively constituted, and what elements of sensemaking are present to facilitate plausible meaning in these interactions?

The tenets of CCO theory and the CSM framework indicate here that the question of plausibility, or the constitution of legitimate identity within and outside of the group, is key. One important element of socially mediated communication which speaks to both the context in which communication flows and the formative context in which sensemaking happens, is the phenomenon of intertextuality. Intertextuality reflects "the way in which a text draws on other texts and discourses" (Hardy, 2004, p. 22). As Vaara, Tienari, and Laurila (2006) explain, it is this structured collection of texts – the comprehensive experience of these interrelated texts, that constructs social reality (Phillips & Hardy, 2002; Barros, 2014).

The interrelatedness of texts in this construction of reality occurs through several distinct processes. Reisigl and Wodak (2001) identify these process for us in terms of intertextuality, interdiscursivity and finally recontextualization. Through social media technologies, these three processes have transformed not only through the speed at which they can occur, but the exploded range of possibilities in terms of how meanings may be connected, changed, translated and taken up by multiple and diverse audiences.

Intertextuality, as described by Bennet (2018, p. 146) refers to a process where "texts are linked diachronically to other texts via content, style, and genre and synchronically via reference to, and the presence of, other discourses."

In their work on textuality and discourse, Reisigl and Wodak (2001) introduce two distinct forms of intertextuality, both of which have implications for our understandings of hyper-textuality in social media. The first is the explicit relationship between texts. This is described as a surface level connection, and represents the "implicit thematic chains that relate texts to each other via underlying assumptions and presuppositions" (p. 185).

Barros (2014) suggests that social media has transformed traditional processes which produced intertextuality to the point where existing narratives and socio-historical discourses can now transform each other through interaction in different ways. The volume of discursive material available, the speed at which it is accessible and the ability of multiple actors to extract cues from this material at once all impact the way that intertextuality unfolds online. In his work on social media technology and intertextuality, Barros (2014) uses critical discourse analysis to investigate the manner in which intertextuality occurred in the case of a Brazilian corporation, Petrobras, that set out to use social media to achieve discursive resistance to combat consistently negative coverage by the traditional mass media. By investigating how texts interacted, drew on one another, and ultimately became transformed via social media, Barros identified a new form of intertextuality referred to as 'hyper-intertextuality.'

> Hyper-intertextuality is the construction of more immediate, intense, and transparent links between texts. For instance, the original design of the Web structure, through the virtual element of hypertext, already allows individual texts to be instantaneously linked to a multiplicity of other discourses.
>
> (Barros, 2014, p. 27)

Barros continues on to describe how hyper-textuality reflects the core elements of intertextuality as described by Hardy (2004), with the addition of differences in speed, transparency, temporality and multiplicity. From a hyper-textuality perspective this may relate to the location of texts on designated Web pages, for example, or the mapping of documents, images and video following click-throughs across tabs. This relationship may also transcend a specific platform or page and ultimately refer to thematic chains across multiple platforms, transforming text within multimedia presentations. In addition, texts can be edited, transformed, combined or deconstructed via social media platforms in an asynchronous format. This both limits and changes the context that an organization or network can put around that text, and calls into action others in the network to either maintain or deconstruct texts as they are introduced.

Interdiscursivity, as described by Bennett (2018), reflects the presence of multiple discourses and genres within a single text. According to Reisigl and Wodak (2001) this means "both the mutual relationships of discourses and the connection, intersecting or overlapping of different discourses 'within' a particular heterogeneous product" (p. 37). This phenomenon is reflected within the social media context through the interactivity of discursive engagement found in chat groups, for example, or comments which follow posts. Interdiscursivity may also be reflected throughout a particular corporate webpage and its supporting social media channels. For example, discourses of nationalism, capitalism and globalization may all be present and overlapping within one government Web presence, supporting a particular initiative or position. Within the new media environment, these discourses may be constructed as multi-platform narratives across a variety of formats, and with varying degrees of interactivity.

Van Leeuwen and Wodak (1999, p. 96) describe a further form of interaction among discourse labeled recontextualization. This is "a principle for appropriating other discourses and bringing them into a special relation with each other for the purpose of their selection, transmission and acquisition." The transformation that occurs within recontextualization is essentially a process of recontextualizing social and discursive practices to "represent (report, explain, analyze, teach, interpret, dramatize, critique etc.) some other social practice(s)" (Van Leeuwen & Wodak, 1999, p. 96). Through recontextualization "texts (and the discourses and genres which they deploy) move between spatially and temporally different contexts, and are subject to transformations whose nature depends upon relationships and differences between such contexts" (Wodak & Fairclough, 2010, p. 22)

Bennett (2018) reminds us, however, that this process of recontextualization is not 'value neutral' and as a result the discursive strategies employed to present this newly contextualized content can have significant implications for their meaning. For example, the use of loaded phrases, tropes and implications can lead the audience to take up a very different message than found in the original text. Wodak and Fairclough (2010, p. 24) caution that the operationalization of recontextualized practices "depends upon 'how they are taken up within particular strategies'."

Moving this concept of recontextualization onto the digital landscape, Bennett (2018) refers to a digitally enabled version of recontextualization, labeled hyper-recontextualization. Like hyper-intertextuality described previously, hyper-recontextualization refers to a form of recontextualization of text that allows for online connections and real-time editing between users and consumers.

Although these forms of textual and discursive interconnectedness are present across all forms of media production, and across multiple platforms, Bennet concludes "that it is this potential for hyper-intertextuality and hyper-recontextualization that marks Twitter as a unique site of discourse (re)production; the format allows for instantaneous recontextualization and reinterpretation of social practices and of discourses, and this in turn is a powerful method of legitimation" (Bennett, 2018, p. 147).

It is in the interconnections between the production and enactment of discourse through texts (in all its forms) that language, power and identity converge to both produce and reflect a shared meaning. This process is not linear; the discursive or truth effects of the language can be privileged in multiple ways, or not at all, depending on the often competing effects of discourses, rules, contexts and meaning in organizations. However, as Mills and Helms Mills indicate,

> to untangle the 'way things are done' in a given place it is important to unravel the various interconnections; too many 'quick-fix' models falsely suggest that it is possible to overcome deep-rooted attitudes and behaviors in a short space of time.
>
> (Helms Mills & Mills, 2000, p. 70)

Critical sensemaking informs us that individuals do not limit their inter-pretation of meaning solely to the language and experiences provided by the organization. The process is much more complex than that, as individuals draw on broader contexts in order to extract cues that support their own sensemaking. This connection between the local site of sensemaking and a broader social context is an important link in the analysis of individual enactment of discourse. Weick et al. (2005, p. 419) point out that the micro-level actions created through sensemaking processes "are small actions with large consequences." Within the social media context, this point is ampli-fied as micro-level communication through individual posts, like, shares, etc., can lead to large consequences within and beyond the network. For example, an inappropriate text sent outside of work time and place can have disciplinary implications for an employee back in the workplace. As local sensemaking happens within a broader context, the linkage between local action and discursive effects on the level of grand discourse cannot be overlooked. From Foucault's poststructuralist perspective, "all knowledge is a selective process that essentially ignores vast areas of the world around it, in order to achieve closure of meaning and come up with a representa-tion of the world that is both purposeful and manageable" (Chan, 2000, p. 1068). The process through which individuals make sense of knowledge by privileging some and ignoring others contributes to this management of meaning. Through the everyday enactment of meaning, individuals within organizations essentially reproduce, create and maintain the broader level societal discourse in which they operate.

In terms of critical sensemaking, the formative context represents a restric-tive influence on organizational rules and individual enactment of meaning through the privileging of these dominant assumptions. Formative contexts, and the related organizational rules, are both productive of, and produced through discourse. In turn, "discourses are related to, and produced by, bodies of knowledge that govern, constrain, and energize people within par-ticular fields" (Treleaven & Sykes, 2005, p. 357).

The importance of this relationship between discursive power and legiti-macy is significant in the enactment of meaning. As Weick et al. (2005, p. 416) advises, "when people face an unsettling difference, that difference often translates into questions such as who are we, what are we doing, what matters, and why does it matter? These are not trivial questions."

This framework offers important insight into why some meanings are acted upon in the process of organizational sensemaking while others are not. Miller (2004, p. 212) explains that "sensemaking is both an individual psychological process (belief-driven by recipes) and an interactive social process (action-driven through communication cycles)." This dual process of understanding and communicating is central to the micro-level enactment of, and therefore the production, maintenance and constraint of, macro-level discourse.

Helms Mills (2003, p. 198) explains enactment as a property of sensemak-ing which "means that we create an activity that reflects our making sense of the experience within our environment." Critical sensemaking draws on organizational rules theory (Mills & Murgatroyd, 1991) to offer an analysis of how these actions are determined. Organization rules focus on "activities of socialization, whereby employees enact organizational rules and maintain organizational culture" (Helms Mills, 2003, p. 199). However, the rules also set limitations on individual sensemaking and actions. This connection between the social construction of beliefs and their creation of, or constraint of actions, is important to the analysis of the enactment of the discourse of change in this study.

In addition to this, the sensemaking properties may influence individual sensemaking simultaneously. For example, the property of enactment may become visible in a particular sensemaking process, but that same enactment of language may influence the plausibility of the language of change, and simultaneously the construction of individual identity. As Helms Mills (2003) states, "if the other six properties are about influences on sensemaking, enactment is about imposing that sense on action" (p. 174).

In this chapter I suggest that enactment as a sensemaking property conducted through social media technologies unfolds differently than in earlier examples of this phenomenon. Because of the way in which social media technologies operate, enactment here can address both the production of text (in a variety of forms) and the physical sharing of the text, the 'taking up' of other cues and the actions associated with a given meaning. As Treem and Leonardi (2013) suggest, "social media are of important consequence to organizational communication processes because they afford behaviors that were difficult or impossible to achieve in combination before these new technologies entered the workplace" (p. 143). Essentially, enacted sensemaking may look different through social media than in non-digital organizational environments. It may also occur at a much faster rate of speed. Cues in the environment occur more rapidly and are much more readily available to the sensemaker. Therefore, the process of sensemaking itself may become truncated as individuals work to restore meaning and routine.

Enactment within sensemaking in any organizational environment further references the issue of power. The question of organizational power and resistance to it has been a primary focus of organizational communication scholars over the past several decades. The advent of social media technologies has focused this discussion even more, as issues of message control, surveillance and access to technological resources come to the forefront. Treem et al. (2013) provide a summary of the literature covering approaches to organizational power, indicating two main streams. The first is a resource dependency view of power "exploring the asymmetry in distribution of organizational resources (e.g. knowledge, information, money, social capital) and the power dependencies they create" (Conrad, 1983; Pfeffer & Davis-Blake, 1987; Scott, 2004) (p. 174).

The second is a critical-cultural stance on power, described by Treem et al. (2013, p. 174) as "power is exercised through the enactment and perpetuation of organizational discourse that privileges the interests of some and marginalizes the voices of others" (Deetz, 1992; Deetz & Mumby, 1985; Mumby & Stohl, 1991).

Next, Treem et al. (2013) summarize the three processes identified in the relationship between power and organizational communication: resource dependencies, surveillance and discursive construction. Resource dependency within a social media context refers to the way in which the knowledge contained in social media is made accessible, or restricted from access, depending upon the audience, the organization and the technology. Access to this knowledge, if it is perceived as valuable, "can be a source of power that can result in increased influence in decision making" (Pfeffer & Salancik, 1974 cited in Treem et al., 2013, p. 175). Social media technologies are evolving so rapidly in the current communication landscape that access to information can be as much a challenge as an opportunity. Although security breaches are certainly not unheard of, many organizations have become quite competent at 'hiding' knowledge from audiences behind paywalls and encryption. This access to knowledge reflects power relationships that must be negotiated through capitalist transactions or access to a dominant coalition.

The next process reviewed here in terms of organizational power is that of surveillance. Research interest in management applications of technology to monitor the work of employees has a long-standing tradition (i.e. Attewell, 1987). Recent advances in the availability and capabilities of social media technology have increased this interest in the boundaries within which individuals and organizations may gather information about each other. Most notably, employee use of social media is an area of contention for many employers and as indicated by Brown and Lightfoot (2002), visible participation via communications technology carries with it a form of accountability on the part of the communicator. To that end, the work of Treem et al. (2013) calls for further research to explore the processes by which individuals monitor the social media activity of coworkers.

Both the access to knowledge and the surveillance views of power address the issue of visibility within the network. From a CSM perspective, the visibility of one's sensemaking is an important element in the process. As Treem et al. (2013, p. 150) point out, "social media afford users the ability to make their behaviors, knowledge, preferences, and communication network connections that were once invisible (or at least very hard to see) visible to others."

As sensemaking is a social and ongoing process, it is very difficult for individuals to collectively make sense of an event or idea if they are limited in their abilities to see how others are making sense of it as well. In fact, one of the principle tenets of sensemaking is the premise that we cannot know what we think until we hear what we say (Weick et al., 2005). Arguably, one of the critical functions of social media is not just to make our work visible to others in the network, but to simultaneously make it visible to ourselves.

In addition to the visibility afforded through social media, enactment is enhanced as well by the editability of our sensemaking – the accessibility of our sensemaking to others who may edit, comment, revise or endorse the plausibility of our narrative.

At the same time, enactment is not limited to the physical production of content for distribution. It is also concerned with the discursive focus of meaning. Correspondingly, work on organizational power has also come from a critical-cultural tradition where scholars are primarily concerned with participation in discursive construction. Work in this vein "views power as constituted by discursive formations created and reproduced in practice (Mumby, 1987)" cited in Treem et al., 2013, p. 175. As Treem et al. explain,

> Social media, by facilitating visible text, can be viewed as an inherently discursive space where individuals are able to put forth arguments and engage in public deliberation. In such studies, researchers are interested in how everyday talk (discourse with a small d) shapes and sustains broader ideologies (Discourse with a big D) and how powerful actors marginalize the contributions of other forms of discourse so as to maintain their positions of power (Alvesson & Deetz, 1999). Studies of social media in organizations have noted that the visibility of content is seen as an effective way for employees to get a feel for what is happening in an organization (Brzozowski, 2009; Jackson, Firtko, & Edenborough, 2007; Zhao & Rosson, 2009).
>
> (Treem et al., 2013, p. 177)

Foucault's (1976) work on discursive power, as discussed in previous chapters, also emphasizes the power-knowledge relationship. This is described as a mutually constitutive process in which "power produces knowledge and discourse and knowledge have power and truth effects" (Leclercq-Vandelannoitte, 2011, p. 1252). The emphasis in this understanding of power is that it both privileges and is privileged through discourse, and it only functions within a dynamic and changing sensemaking environment. "Power must be analyzed as something that circulates . . . that functions only when it is part of a chain. It is never localized here or there, it is never in the same hands. . . . Power is exercised through networks" (Foucault, 1976, p. 98).

Ultimately, power in this form exists to impose order on society, and therefore the notion of discursive struggle is central to the literature on power and discourse (Hardy & Phillips, 1999). Within this literature actors use text to challenge or destabilize discourse.

Actors use 'texts as weapons' to challenge the other's dominant position (Hardy & Phillips, 2004). Barros (2014, p. 1212) applies this notion of discursive resistance using text as tools to investigate the ways in which new media technologies can offer new discursive tools that enhance or enable an actor's ability to challenge dominant discourse.

Nevertheless, although new digital technologies may facilitate the use of textual tools, the social media networks in which they operate have become more complex. As Rouse (2005, p. 109) explains

> power is dispersed across complicated and heterogeneous social networks marked by ongoing struggle. Power is not something present at specific locations within those networks, but is instead always at issue in ongoing attempts to (re)produce effective social alignments, and conversely to avoid or erode their effects, often by producing various counter alignments. . . . Power can thus never be simply present, as one action forcibly constraining or modifying another. Its constitution as a power relation depends upon its re-enactment or reproduction over time as a sustained power relationship.

It is this constant state of flux which operates across social media networks that makes understandings of power and resistance within the digital environment so challenging. As sensemaking encourages individuals to establish routines and create meanings that restore order to their networks, the way in which texts interact with each other and reconstitute themselves discursively makes the process virtually impossible.

Drawing again on the Foucauldian notion of power, Leclercq-Vandelannoitte (2011, p. 1255) explains that

> power relationships evolve, because they are situational, contextualized, mobile and sometimes conflicting. Perpetual interactions characterize the relationships of discourses, discipline and structures, as well as subjectification, identities and individual reactions in the ongoing organizing stream. These interrelationships enable organizations to be produced and reproduced and transformed continually. For example, this dynamic approach can reconceptualise the concept of technology, positioned as part of the process in which technology, organization and subjects become redefined.

The dynamic relationships which both produce and are productive of power in the processes of organizing and organization mean that power cannot exist without the presence of resistance. As Leclercq-Vandelannoitte summarizes, "Discourses are simultaneously sites of domination and resistance and involved in the deconstruction and reconstruction of organizations" (Leclercq-Vandelannoitte, 2011, p. 1252). As power operates within a system, resistance cannot exist outside of power – only within this same process of constant becoming, organizing and making sense.

Resistance within the social media context highlights this Foucauldian understanding of power. Discourses of resistance function here in systems of technology with the aim to destabilize dominant discourses of power. Social media technologies have been credited with great potential for the democratization of information in response to a corporate-controlled mainstream media industry (Carroll & Hackett, 2006). Although more recent work has indicated that social media ought not to be credited in total for the sweep of resistance movements unfolding in the last decade, there is agreement that these technologies do offer the possibility under some circumstances to transform access to power-knowledge networks, resulting in what Innocent Chiluwa (2012) refers to as a 'discourse of resistance.'

We also see in the literature on social movements and digital media that the discursive space between the dominant narrative at the local level and the broader social discourse it reflects can result in a plurality of outcomes in terms of sensemaking and enactment. This space appears to be most visible in the area of identity construction. In the case of the social organizing discussed earlier, the contribution of individual actions to organizational sensemaking becomes apparent. The impact of these enactments of meaning is highlighted in the way in which discourse is translated into local practices.

In the following chapter I look at a case study featuring the #marchagainstMonsanto protest event and associated social networks. The primary social media platform utilized in this movement was Twitter. As indicated previously, Twitter offers a unique space in which collective sensemaking can happen for several reasons, including as Bennett (2018) describes, the potential for hyper-intertextuality and hyper-recontextualization. Twitter itself is used most effectively through its multi-platform capacity for storytelling. Although the length of text is very limited, tweets can include directions and maps to sensemaking through hyperlinks, embedded video, imagery and signposts in the form of hashtags and handles. In the previous case study on Volkswagen, the importance of the designated hashtag (#dieselgate) became evident as both a cue and a discursive strategy defining the nature of the scandal. In the case of #MarchAgainstMonsanto the designated hashtag again offers a discursive position, but also makes a call for action. The element of mobilization behind this signpost indicates a particular kind of enactment as well as the nature of the organization. Likewise, the use of a designated hashtag connects individual Twitter users to a broader 'conversation.' The simple addition of that discursive element within the text of a tweet (message) changes the nature of that contribution from a single message from a single user, to a part of a much larger and collective conversation that transcends barriers of time and location. I am also interested in the connection between the Twitter platform and enactment of sensemaking as Twitter is arguably one of the most mobile of social media platforms. It is designed for use on mobile devices and used almost exclusively in that forum. The mobility aspect of this technology may have interesting implications for not only the recontextualization of text but the extraction of cues and social nature of sensemaking as well. I was originally drawn to the Monsanto example as I searched for insight into the growing use of social media to enact and legitimize social movements online. In this case study we will see that the size and reach of the network, the number of influencers in that network and the durability of the message all contributed to a plausible legitimation of the emerging grassroots organization.

10 #MarchAgainstMonsanto – social movements, extracting cues and the ongoing nature of sensemaking

This chapter focuses on the mobilization of social movements via social media from a Critical Sensemaking perspective. The durability of these movements through social media and overtime highlight them as interesting forms of organizing and of sensemaking. In the example of one controversial social initiative, #MarchAgainstMonsanto, the organizational identity of a multinational corporation is challenged by an emerging identity constructed through social interaction. Of particular interest within this process is the crafting of narratives that construct meanings around engagement and enactment, while at the same time highlighting cues from a complex communication environment. The text produced through this initiative reflects both narrative data at a particular point in time, as well as an ongoing conversation or narrative construction. Through communicative processes, key influencers in the social media networks enroll individuals into a growing social media network, and enlarge the reach and range of messages. At the same time, the messages themselves evolve and are re-constituted or co-constituted as they are shared and re-tweeted to the network.

The multinational corporation Monsanto represents itself as a sustainable agriculture company, delivering agricultural products that support farmers all around the world. This identity is contested, however, by others who contend it is a company aggressively monopolizing the trade in seeds and herbicides (Spijkers, 2016)

In 2013, a mother in Utah named Tami Canal became so fed up and outraged with the practices of Monsanto and implications for healthy food, that she started what became an international movement, #MarchAgainstMonsanto. May 2018 will see the 7th annual march. Hundreds of thousands of participants are expected, with events happening in over 500 cities worldwide.

As Canal describes, she was essentially looking for an outlet for her frustration around GMOs. What started out as posts on a Facebook page and blog turned into a more organized effort to raise awareness. In an interview in 2013, she says she hoped the initiative

"would go nationwide but my initial goal was 3,000, I never thought it would get this big. I thought if I could get 3,000 people to join me (on

May 25) that would be a success. I marched in Utah and I said even if it would only be myself out there, I don't care if I look like a psycho, I will be handing out fliers; it means that much to me that people know what's really going on"

(Meyer, 2013, para. 21)

The event that year turned out to be more successful than she could have imagined. On the March against Monsanto website the group is described as "an international grassroots movement and protest against Monsanto corporation."

In her 2013 interview, Canal further described the grassroots organization that formed to get the first event off the ground as including support of a small group that was very instrumental in it being so successful; Emily, a freelance journalist from Seattle, and Nick of the Anti-Media webpage, were very willing to jump in and help.

> We also had the support of a rebel digital anarchy group based in Europe. . . . A lot of people were turned off by us working with anarchists but that's why we were so successful, we didn't turn away anybody because food affects everyone regardless of your political or religious affiliations, etc. The group was called 'A Revolt: Digital Anarchy' and they're actually an incredibly peaceful group.

(Meyer, 2013, para. 5)

Although the march and its message were successful in raising awareness, not everyone agreed that the message was credible. As Qaim (2016) summarizes,

> NGOs have successfully framed GMOs as something inherently evil, and this evil is epitomized by Monsanto. This becomes very obvious by NGO-initiated movements named 'Operation Cremate Monsanto' or 'March against Monsanto' (Herring, 2006; March against Monsanto, 2015), which are quite militant in their activities yet entice a sizeable community of followers.

(p. 136)

This case, as we saw in the #dieselgate example, highlights the importance of the designated hashtag as a textual constitution of organization and an artifact of sensemaking. As texts which influence sensemaking, hashtags operate as cues which extract meaning from a crowded environment. The # combined with a keyword or phrase acts as a "bottom-up user-proposed tagging convention" (Chang, 2010, p. 1). By including a specific hashtag, the user identifies communicatively with an idea or organization and indicates association with that conversation. This enactment of sensemaking, reflecting both a textual representation of the keyword and a sorting process, allows for organized extraction of cues. This tagging process also contributes to the construction of legitimacy in the network, as the designated hashtag indicates a sense of connection and endorsement through a shared identifier.

Sensemaking is focused on and by extracted cues. By extracting cues, individuals are engaged in an ongoing process of focusing on certain elements, while completely ignoring others, in order to support their interpretation of an event. Since sensemaking is retrospective, past experiences, including rules and regulations, dictate what cues we will extract to make sense of a situation (Helms Mills et al., 2010, p. 185).

From a critical perspective, individuals also bring a degree of agency to the cue selection process, yet the possible range of choices which are plausible and legitimate is constrained by the broader context. Simply because a hashtag is trending does not mean that an individual will choose to adopt it and engage in a communication process around it. But it does put that cue on the table, so to speak, and as that information, combined with other elements of organizing are made sense of, the individual may choose to join the trending network.

The social element of sensemaking also brings considerable weight to bear on the process. As an item is privileged on Twitter as trending, it embodies a social presence that may contribute to its legitimacy. And as the topic (and corresponding symbolic designation) begins to successfully carve out space as a distinctive voice within a sea of other hashtags, that hashtag may emerge as authentic.

And as in any organization, members of the Twitter network are governed by rules for organizing, often termed Twitter etiquette. These include rules and best practices, for example, on how to use Twitter appropriately for debate, discussion and real-time evaluation of ideas (Pemmaraju, Mesa, Majhail, and Thompson (2017). These rules also include the boundaries established by the technological structures which define the platform. For example, messages are limited to 140 characters, etc.

In May 2013 the strategy for legitimation adopted by #MarchAgainstMonsanto was to utilize a particular form of strategic Twitter communication called the Twitterstorm.

A Twitterstorm is a sudden and focused spike in activity surrounding a certain topic on the Twitter social media site. It can be started by a single individual or a group, sending out to his or her followers a message often related to breaking news or a controversial debate. Using a certain and often original hashtag, the tweet quickly spreads as people are notified of the message and then reuse the hashtag with subsequent re-tweets and tweets.

According to Techopedia, when a specific tweet and hashtag are tweeted and re-tweeted quickly enough, the hashtag is included on Twitter's "trending" list and displayed to all Twitter users, even those who are not a member of the hashtag user's list of followers. This often leads to the original message or hashtag crossing to other social media sites or the mainstream media, resulting in much deeper penetration into the collective conscience.

Precise, a UK-based business information monitoring group, suggests there are three types of Twitterstorms:

1 The perfect Twitterstorm: Starts on Twitter, is picked up by traditional press through various feedback loops and reaches a wide audience, even those who are not on Twitter.
2 The storm in a cup: A story that generates a relatively small interest on Twitter but is picked up by traditional media, so it still garners quite a wide audience. This usually occurs when the mainstream media attempts to anticipate online trends before they actually occur.
3 The Twitter-only storm: A story that gains a significant volume of attention on Twitter but only might be of interest to a specific group and is not picked up by mainstream media (Twitterstorm, 2018, para 4).

The group messaged its followers on Twitter and Facebook:

> The March Against Monsanto is launching a global 'Twitter storm' at 9PM EST on Saturday 10/5/13. The goal of this Twitter storm is to get the March and info about GMOs trending on Twitter and Facebook and to build awareness about Monsanto and their dangerous products and policies. We are asking people to tweet and post certain hash tags as frequently as possible between the hours of 9PM EST and 10PM EST (6–7PM PST).

In this example of resistance through social media, there was use of a Twitterstorm which essentially functioned to raise awareness and move a discussion out of its own limited discussion group, into other network conversations. This is achieved through trending. Trending occurs when the hashtags that are most widely used at any given time appear in the Twitter navigation sidebar as trending topics.

Trending is particularly effective on Twitter as a communication platform because it is essentially designed for mobility and to operate in real-time (Zhao & Rosson, 2009). In contrast to other asynchronous platforms such as blogs, or Facebook, Twitter is designed for immediacy and real-time interaction, therefore social networking is not Twitter's sole utility; it is widely used for real-time content sharing (Chang, 2010). This facility lends itself to the communicative processes necessary for a logic of aggregation (Juris, 2012), as discussed in the previous chapter. This ability to engage individuals in a process of organizing with branches in both online and physical spaces is useful from a CSM perspective as it manages a fairly diverse sensemaking environment with 'rules' for both online and public spaces.

The formative context in which #MarchAgainstMonsanto exists is further constrained by organizational rules. In this case, the rules of organizing also include rules of engagement with the technological structures. For example, all participants are to use the #MarchAgainstMonsanto as they participate in the Twitterstorm and participation is bound by time constraints.

In order to visually analyze the network surrounding #MarchAgainst-Monsanto, data from Twitter was gathered for a two-week period in 2015, just prior to that year's march. This included the Twitterstorm strategy and represented a conversation focused on raising awareness of the event and translating that awareness into offline engagement.

The network map gathered using Netlytic.org indicated that the nodes and edges of the network provide some interesting insights into how individuals are interacting. The centralized nature of the communication shows that the key message originates from one, or a very limited number of clusters, i.e. through the organizing group, and then re-tweeted or shared throughout the network and out into other networked spaces. It is interesting to note, there is not a great deal of interactive, two-way communication in this network. In this case, and as is consistent with the objective to create a Twitterstorm, the purpose was to disseminate messages as widely as possible, so that the hashtag itself would start trending, thus drawing the attention of otherwise unconnected Twitter users.

This visualization indicates that the designated hashtag was quite successful at starting conversations amongst users, who were tweeting and re-tweeting the hashtag, and in that way becoming part of the evolving organization. There is not a strong indicator of two-way communication from the main nodes; however, it is visually apparent that individual users are communicating to one another. The objective here is an outward push of the hashtag to raise awareness and create interest across a broad range of networks. The message in this network is quite centralized, but the question of whether the related organization functions that way is another matter. From a CCO perspective, these various communicative strategies in and of themselves do not necessarily constitute organization.

As Putnam and Nicotera (2009) argue, the four flows of communication described in the CCO approach do not necessarily constitute organization without attention to coordinated action, co-orientation and/or the constitution of authority (p. 3). Although McPhee and Zaug's (2009) Four Flows approach has been critiqued for not providing a clear definition of the differences between what constitutes an organization and what is alternatively a community, a network or a group (i.e. Sillince, 2010; Bisel, 2010), Putnam and Nicotera (2009) emphasize that the Four Flows approach describes a complex process of organizing. "The four flows interface and are interwoven in complex ways to constitute an organization" (Putnam & Nicotera, 2009, p. 4). In this way, a network, for example, could enact the four flows of communication in such a way as to constitute organization, and at the same time accomplish organizing. In the case of the March against Monsanto, the network moved rapidly in its formation through an individual process of sensemaking, embodied in resistance to a dominant corporate narrative.

In terms of local and offline organizing, the marches often take place in conjunction with, or under the auspices of, other similarly minded local organizations. For example, The Adelaide (Australia) March Against Monsanto rally was organized as a project of Friends of the Earth (FoE), Adelaide's 'Fair Food Adelaide' collective. It built momentum for a continuation of a GM-ban across South Australia (SA), and pressure to implement this ban in other states. As their online material describes, "SA is the only mainland state to have a moratorium on commercial GM, but food labeling and testing are currently inadequate and we want that to change. The rally was joined by SA's Minster for Agriculture Leon Bignell, Senator Nick Xenophon and Greens MLC Mark Parnell. *More information: www.march-against-monsanto.com – Robyn Wood, FoE Adelaide. FOE chain reaction*" (FoE, 2014, Homepage).

This case again highlights how offline events can influence online organizing. The first marches against Monsanto occurred in the United States two days after Senate Amendment 965, introduced by US Senator Bernie Sanders allowing states to label GMO foods, was defeated (Upton, 2013). Founder Cami Tamal suggests that event may have been one of the cues for participants in 2013, to tip support for the first march over the top.

11 Conclusion

Throughout the preceding chapters I have offered some impressions on the ways in which social media communication is transforming our sensemaking around organization and identity. Here I will draw some conclusions on the questions this poses with regard to socially constructed organizational identities and suggest some paths for future scholarship in this area.

In the introduction to this discussion I took as a starting point that social media construct a reality where networks, artifacts, actors, meanings and identities converge without the traditional limitations of time and space (Gilpin et al., 2010; Fuchs, 2005). The volume of information available through this media, its persistence and its frenzied nature create a challenging landscape for communicators concerned with authenticity and organizational identity. At the same time, individuals and organizations are challenged to very rapidly extract cues and enact a sensemaking environment defined by 'flux.' The production and consumption of text, in its many forms, through these networks emphasizes the intertextuality, and in fact the hyper-textuality, discussed in earlier chapters. This transformation in the very nature of text and the discursive effects that it produces offers a rich site of investigation for future scholarship.

In that sense, social media technologies are more than just channels of communication, they actually transform communication – through which organizations are constituted. The elusive nature of how social media function makes it difficult to determine a clear and fixed definition either of these technologies or of their roles in organizations and society. I began by defining social media in Chapter 1 while acknowledging that there is no consensus within the literature on exactly what the category of social media defines, nor as to how social media is used. As a first step, I used Kaplan and Haenlein's (2010) definition of social media as "a group of internet-based applications that build on the ideological and technological foundations of Web 2.0, and that allow the creation and exchange of user generated content" (p. 61). As they further point out, however, the broad term of social media has been applied to a wide variety of technologies which are rapidly emerging, converging and re-imaging themselves in a dynamic technological environment (Kaplan & Haenlein, 2010).

As evidenced throughout this volume, even though this definition allows for the complexities of labeling these technologies, the problem is even more challenging. In the examples analyzed throughout this book we see that the way these technologies function changes more than just how we communicate, but also who we are. As individuals collectively question who are we, and how are things done here, social media provide access to a broader range of possible and plausible alternatives, as they conversely provide constraints to our sensemaking that emerge from multiple and diverse interests. Each of the examples further serve to highlight the ways in which Weick's (1995) seven properties of sensemaking influence collective sensemaking both on and offline. In particular, the sensemaking properties of plausibility, enactment and identity construction emerge as the key components in collective, digital sensemaking, although other properties, such as the focusing on and extracting of cues, occur 'behind the scenes' and simultaneously to strengthen or determine sensemaking alternatives.

In concert with the property of plausibility, understandings of legitimacy in a variety of forms is an important piece of the social media interaction – legitimacy is experienced in this environment as variations of authenticity, legitimation and plausibility or in some cases, trust. Social understandings of authenticity, as described in Chapter 5 have shifted over time. The historical meaning of this term implied that to live an authentic life was seen as both being true to oneself, and also engaging in a form of society where democratic process made it possible for one to live one's own authentic life. This connection to participative democracy, where an individual's right to an authentic life hinges on the protection of the rights of others for that same opportunity, has been eroded over time. The cluttered and competitive social media environment positions authenticity as an ability to carve out a distinctive voice within a crowded communicative space. The ability of organizations to do this in terms of imprinting an identity on sensemaking, on- and offline, contributes to the plausibility of its narrative. As more users and networks engage with the online world, this struggle to surface distinctive and 'authentic' narratives above the noise of the crowd will continue to challenge organizations and professional communicators. The existing scholarship on narrative in sensemaking may be useful here as social media platforms are designed most effectively for the purpose of constructing and sharing narratives on an individual, organizational and global level.

As we considered these challenges, we further investigated the physical constraints to sensemaking found offline, time and space, which are typically seen as unnecessary or unimportant in social media communication. However, the examples here have shown that in some cases, time and space are key to successful organizing and identity construction. For instance, the ability to transcend or at least navigate interconnections between digital spaces and physical public spaces underlies the power of social media to activate elements of identity in both worlds. And time-bound communication like the WOL (working out loud) experience on Twitter, the creation of a Twitterstorm or the use of social media like twitter or Snapchat to facilitate ongoing real-time communication relate social media communication very directly to offline events and experiences which are happening simultaneously.

I did not look too deeply into the implications of time-determined sensemaking or the impact of time and space on the communicative process. However, this is an interesting and important area, and I think it will prove to be very relevant to work situated within the social media milieu.

In his work on temporal sensemaking, Eldon Wiebe (2010) directs us to an expanding literature that suggests sensemaking may not be limited to retrospection. Part of this trend toward a different understanding of retrospective sensemaking may be related to an evolution of our understanding of time. Weibe suggests that our traditional reliance on 'clock time' actually may obscure our sensemaking around what is actually happening temporally. He points out that individuals within organizations may not be truly aware of their relationship with time. He continues that, "time is not singular nor is it an invariant constant" (Purser et al., 2005 cited in Wiebe, 2010, p. 214). Adam (1994, p. 509) observed that even within Western culture the dominance of clock time "does not obliterate the rich sources of local, idiosyncratic and context-dependent time-awareness that are rooted in the social and organic rhythms of everyday life." Likewise, Hall (1983, p. 13) observed that in "looking at what people actually do (in contrast to what they write and say when theorizing) one quickly discovers a wide discrepancy between time as it is lived and time as it is considered" (p. 214).

In his work, Wiebe (2010) refers to the process of seeking to understand how time is used by managers to frame the change they are experiencing as temporal sensemaking. By temporal sensemaking he means "the act of configuring (and reconfiguring) the relationship of past, present and future" (p. 216). Weibe takes for his starting point in this process Emirbayer and Mische's (1998) reconceptualization of human agency as:

> a temporally embedded process of social engagement, informed by the past (in its habitual aspect), but also oriented toward the future (as a capacity to imagine alternative possibilities) and toward the present (as a capacity to contextualize past habits and future projects within the contingencies of the moment). (Emirbayer & Mische, 1998, p. 963).
>
> From a sensemaking perspective, this definition suggests that actors can construct the flow of time in which they locate themselves, influencing not only the processes of retrospection, but arguably the bracketing which occurs around the sensemaking process itself.

Along with an increased focus on organizational sensemaking, the CCO perspective is also gaining traction among public relations scholars as it allows for an integration around some key insights. Most notably, identifying the ways in which understandings of organizations and organizational events as communicatively constituted can inform individual engagement in processes of organizing. From that perspective organizational identities emerge as durable and persist within and beyond the organization. These identities are understood to be created and maintained in language, not actions or results (Grant et al., 1998). Thus, a company's identity may be formed with rhetoric, not tangible results of management processes (Oswick et al., 2005; Thurlow & Mills, 2009).

Nevertheless, tackling the broader questions of networked identities is a difficult one, and from a CCO perspective this may take one of several different approaches. Throughout this volume the term CCO will represent the phrase *communication is constitutive of organizing* (Putnam & Nicotera, 2009). Bisel (2010) describes the current state of CCO quite succinctly when he says, "CCO theories articulate a communicative ontology of organization. Although the specific mechanisms and processes by which communication is associated with organization are debated hotly among theorists, one premise remains constant across the tradition: Communication calls organization into being" (Bisel, 2010, p. 124).

Although I have discussed the three somewhat distinctive orientations of the CCO approach, the strong commonalities in the foundational assumptions of CCO mean that these may not necessarily be mutually exclusive ways of seeing organizations and identity. There is no doubt that at the core of CCO theory there is agreement on the centrality of language to organization. However, variations in the definition of organization (or organizing) and differences in approach to the role of communicative processes in constituting organization mean the different schools of thought in this theoretical framework are sometimes at odds with each other. As Putnam and Fairhurst (2015) suggest, each of these three understandings had weaknesses that could be addressed by the other two perspectives. They further advocate that theory building should cross perspectives, and encourage the potential in "using the object orientation to address relativism in the becoming approach as well as introducing materiality in the grounded-in-action view" (Putnam & Fairhurst, 2015, p. 377).

Throughout the majority of the examples discussed here, the Montreal School approach has been illustrated, reflecting the work of Taylor and Van Emery (2000) as they argue that organizations emanate from two communicative circumstances, 'conversation' and 'text.' Text understood as a structuring principle which can include any 'stable patterning' or documenting of values, roles or rules which govern the organizational identity. In contrast, 'conversation' is seen as the shared interactions occurring in everyday situations when people come together to coordinate around specific objectives (p. 35). On the other hand, in some examples discussed here, for example, the case of the #MarchAgainstMonsanto and other forms of collective enactment, the insights of the Four Flows approach offered useful insights into the processes of organizing, getting organized and organizational identity as they unfolded in different spaces.

At the same time, there are limits to the applicability of CCO theory to the questions presented by social media. The CCO perspective can provide valuable insights into processes of identity construction within this digital context; however, CCO theory alone does not give us the complete picture. Bisel (2010, p. 129) pointed to the need to expand the work of CCO theory further, so as to acknowledge that communication is a necessary condition for the constitution of organizing, "but it is not sufficient to ensure organizing will be called into being." This call for further work leads us to reflect again on the question posed in Chapter 1, why do some organizational identities persist and become durable, and others do not? What is the communicative condition under which organizations move into becoming, and identities emerge as plausible to prospective or newly enrolled organizational members?

There is potential for further theory building around the integration of CCO theory and the CSM framework. These two approaches together offer synergies that may provide added awareness of the complex relationships between the constraints and potential of the formative context, characterized by discursive power and rules, and the agency afforded individual sensemakers through communicative processes. In uncovering the shocks or communicative events which trigger sensemaking, CCO theory offers some important clues to the process of organization which ensues. Public relations scholars may find useful insights related to the way individuals collectively bracket around shocks in their sensemaking, and the literature on sensemaking during a crisis offers both theoretical and applied experience in this area (i.e. Weick, 1988).

Digital media may represent new channels of communication, yet they are still defined by social processes embedded in conversations, texts, interactions and sensemaking. As a result, social media communication surfaces experiences and interactions that may previously have gone unspoken or undocumented within organizations. For that reason, digital media networks offer a rich site of inquiry for CCO scholars who wish to explore the processes through which organizational identities are formed and maintained through time. And, as new technologies emerge, the ability to navigate and integrate both online and offline spaces will take an increasingly important focus in applications of CCO to the constitution of organization.

Future developments in social media, and the increased role of these technologies in organizational communication may further by informed by Kent and Taylor's (2014) work on the future of social media in public relations. In previous chapters we have reviewed several emergent themes these authors highlight as requiring our attention in the digital media age. The themes were identified through a Delphi technique with a panel of public relations experts who, among other things, highlighted two contradictory elements which in some ways define the challenge of social media authenticity and collective sensemaking. The first is a tendency toward fragmentation; the second is a tendency toward collaboration with like-minded individuals. Fragmentation and collaboration define two ends of the social media spectrum, and these two approaches can work both for and against processes of legitimation. Fragmentation is understood by Kent and Taylor (2014) as a process of dissociation from relationships as communication is increasingly shared in asynchronous environments. This circumstance is compounded by the fact that individuals enrolled in networks through social media are often engaged with such large numbers of 'friends' or 'followers' that the sheer volume of people engaged in any given conversation makes it impossible for deep communication or relationship building. Further complicating this situation, and related to the next challenge, is the likelihood of individuals who express an opposing view to others in the network to be blocked or jettisoned from the conversation. The merging of technological limitations and limited 'real' human interactions leads to a fragmented communication environment where individuals are isolated into silos from the broader public sphere.

Kent and Taylor's (2014) second theme of collaboration, with its insights into the creation of echo chambers in our communicatively constituted environments, reminds us that the potential represented through social media is tempered by the entrenchment of silos where conversations occur in isolation of broader context and dissenting opinion.

> In a well-functioning democracy, people do not live in echo chambers or information cocoons. They see and hear a wide range of topics and ideas. They do so even if they did not, and would not, choose to see and hear those topics and those ideas in advance. These claims raise serious questions about online behavior and uses of social media, and the astonishing growth in the power to choose – to screen in and screen out.
> (Sunstein, 2018, p. xi)

The meta discourses which underpin formative contexts in terms of sensemaking offline, are the same ones that inform and constrain our sensemaking online. The discourse of capitalism, for example, in the case of crowdfunding prevails whether online or offline, and the site of the conversation does not change the discursive power relationship in which it operates. Future study is warranted here to investigate the tension between the e-democratic potential of social media and the discursive power of capitalist development in which it has emerged.

In many cases, the motivation behind crowdsourcing has a social action component. This can be realized in the form of seeking alternative approaches to traditional financing opportunities or garnering support for social justice or community development initiatives. Crowdfunding happens exclusively through social media networks, and in many ways mirrors examples of social activism that are taking place through those same channels. As Kahn and Kellner (2004) point out, there has been a surge of grassroots movements attempting to carry out "globalization from below" in opposition to "the capitalist strategy of globalization-from-above" (p. 89).

Future research in this area must also include further work on the question of agency. Consistent with Townley's (1994, p. 107) caution that "it would be a mistake to assume that the individual is a passive participant in the constitution of identity," the investigation of identity provided within a social media context is concerned with the role of agency in the production and maintenance of those identities.

Through the integration of insights around agency at the micro-level through individual sensemaking, at the meso level through textual and discursive agency, and through the formative context which operates on a societal level, the case studies in this book have touched on agency throughout the identity construction process. One of the key elements emerging from this investigation highlights the ways in which not only human, but non-human actants engaged with agency throughout this process. By drawing on work from Actor Network Theory, Framing Theory, and notions of power which allow for fluidity within networks, the representation of textual agency here pulls together a broad array of tools with which to tackle the constantly evolving nature of text within digital networks.

The perspective in this work has been to address the question of agency through the framework of individual sensemaking in a broader, critical context. While this provides useful insights into how and under what conditions an individual may engage one or more of the sensemaking properties in her construction of meaning, it does not offer a consistent or predictive understanding of how meaning is constituted. Although this may be at the very nature of identity construction, further research in this area may help public relations scholars to understand why some social media 'revolutions' transcend into offline spaces and others do not.

This central question of how organization and organizing is achieved across online and offline space will inform a great deal of our work as public relations scholars in the coming years. Much of what I have argued here is concerned with the need for scholarship in this area to adopt a broader and more critical view of the role of social media technologies in the communicative constitution of organization and, broadly speaking, society. New tools are needed in our investigation of this field, and the application of both CCO and CSM approaches may prove fruitful in the future interrogation of this environment.

References

Adam, B. (1994). Perceptions of time. In *Companion encyclopedia of anthropology* (pp. 503–526). London: Routledge.

Ahrne, G., & Brunsson, N. (2011). Organization outside organizations: The significance of partial organization. *Organization, 18*(1), 83–104.

Albert, S., & Whetten, D. (1985). Organizational identity. In L. Cummings & B. Staw (Eds.), *Research in organizational behavior* (7th ed., pp. 263–295). Greenwich, CT: JAI Press.

Alavi, M., & Leidner, D. E. (2001). Review: Knowledge management and knowledge management systems: Conceptual foundations and research issues. *MIS Quarterly, 25*(1), 107–136.

Albu, O. B., & Etter, M. (2016). Hypertextuality and social media: A study of the constitutive and paradoxical implications of organizational Twitter use. *Management Communication Quarterly, 30*(1), 5–31.

Alexander, J. C., Giesen, B., & Mast, J. L. (2006). Social performance: Symbolic action, cultural pragmatics, and ritual. *Cambridge cultural social studies*. Cambridge: Cambridge University Press.

Alvesson, M., & Deetz, S. (1999). Critical theory and postmodernism: Approaches to organizational studies. *Studying Organization: Theory and Method*, 185–211.

Ashcraft, K. L., Kuhn, T. R., & Cooren, F. (2009). Constitutional amendments: Materializing organizational communication. *The Academy of Management Annals, 3*(1).

Ashforth, B. E., & Gibbs, B. W. (1990). The double-edge of organisational legitimation. *Organisation Science, 1*(2), 177–194.

Aten, K., & Thomas, G. F. (2016). Crowdsourcing strategizing: Communication technology affordances and the communicative constitution of organizational strategy. *International Journal of Business Communication, 53*(2), 148–180.

Attewell, P. (1987). Big brother and the sweatshop: Computer surveillance in the automated office. *Sociological Theory, 5*, 87–100.

Bannerman, S. (2013). Crowdfunding culture. *Journal of Mobile Media, 7*(1), 1–30.

Barlow, J. P. (1996). *A declaration of the independence of cyberspace*. Retrieved May 12, 2017, from www.eff.org/cyberspace-independence

Barros, M. (2014). Tools of legitimacy: The case of the Petrobras corporate blog. *Organisation Studies, 35*(8), 1211–1230.

Bateson, G. (1972). *Steps to an ecology of the mind*. New York, NY: Ballantine.

Benkler, Y. (2006). *The wealth of networks: How social production transforms markets and freedom*. New Haven, CT: Yale University Press.

Bennett, S. (2018). *Constructions of migrant integration in British public discourse: Becoming British*. London: Bloomsbury Publishing.

Bennett, W. L., & Iyengar, S. (2008). A new era of minimal effects? The changing foundations of political communication. *Journal of Communication, 58*(4), 707–731.

Berman, M. (1970). *The politics of authenticity: Radical individualism and the emergence of modern society*. New York, NY: Atheneum.

Bisel, R. S. (2010). A communicative ontology of organization? A description, history, and critique of CCO theories for organization science. *Management Communication Quarterly, 24*(1), 124–131.

Blackler, F. (1992). Formative contexts and activity systems: Postmodern approaches to the management of change. In M. R. A. M. Hughes (Ed.), *Rethinking organization: New directions in organization theory and analysis*. Newbury Park: Sage.

Blaschke, S., Schoeneborn, D., & Seidl, D. (2012). Organizations as networks of communication episodes: Turning the network perspective inside out. *Organization Studies, 33*(7), 879–906.

Blumler, J. G., & Gurevitch, M. (2001). The new media and our political communication discontents: Democratizing cyberspace. *Information, Communication & Society, 4*(1), 1–13.

Boje, D. M. (1991). The storytelling organization: A study of story performance in an office-supply firm. *Administrative Science Quarterly*, 106–126.

Boyd, D. M. (2014). *It's complicated: The social lives of networked teens*. New Haven, CT: Yale University Press.

Boyd, D. M., & Ellison, N. B. (2007). Social network sites: Definition, history, and scholarship. *Journal of Computer-Mediated Communication, 13*(1), 210–230. doi:10.1111/j.1083-6101.2007.00393.x

Brass, D. J., Galaskiewicz, J., Greve, H. R., & Tsai, W. (2004). Taking stock of networks and organizations: A multilevel perspective. *Academy of Management Journal, 47*(6), 795–817.

Brown, A. D. (2000). Making sense of inquiry sensemaking. *Journal of Management Studies, 37*, 45–75.

Brown, S. D., & Lightfoot, G. (2002). Presence, absence, and accountability: E-mail and the mediation of organizational memory. In S. Woolgar (Ed.), *Virtual society? Technology, cyberbole, reality* (pp. 209–229). Oxford, England: Oxford University Press.

Brown, A. D., Stacey, P., & Nandhakumar, J. (2008). Making sense of sensemaking narratives. *Human Relations, 61*(8), 1035–1062.

Browning, L. D., Greene, R. W., Sitkin, S. B., Sutcliffe, K. M., & Obstfeld, D. (2009). Constitutive complexity. *Building Theories of Organization: The Constitutive Role of Communication*, 89–116.

Brummans, B. H. J. M., Cooren, F., Robichaud, D., & Taylor, J. R. (2014). Approaches to the communicative constitution of organizations. *The SAGE Handbook of Organizational Communication: Advances in Theory, Research, and Methods*, 173–194.

Brzozowski, M. J. (2009, May). WaterCooler: Exploring an organization through enterprise social media. In *Proceedings of the ACM 2009 international conference on supporting group work* (pp. 219–228). United States: ACM Association for Computing Machinery.

Burnham, D. (1984). *The rise of the computer state*. New York, NY: Vintage Books.

Butler, B. S. (2001). Membership size, communication activity, and sustainability: A resource based model of online social structures. *Information Systems Research, 12*(4), 346–362.

Cacciatore, M. A., Scheufele, D. A., & Iyengar, S. (2016). The end of framing as we know it . . . and the future of media effects. *Mass Communication and Society, 19*(1), 7–23.

Capella, J., & Jamieson, K. H. (1997). *Spiral of cynicism: The press and the public good.* Oxford, UK: Oxford University Press.

Carroll, W. K., & Hackett, R. A. (2006). Democratic media activism through the lens of social movement theory. *Media, Culture & Society, 28*(1), 83–104.

Chan, A. (2000). Redirecting critique in postmodern organization studies: The perspective of Foucault. *Organization Studies, 21*(6), 1059–1075.

Chang, H. C. (2010). A new perspective on Twitter hashtag use: Diffusion of innovation theory. *Proceedings of the Association for Information Science and Technology, 47*(1), 1–4.

Chia, R. (2000). Discourse analysis as organizational analysis. *Organization, 7*(3), 513–518.

Chiluwa, I. (2012). Social media networks and the discourse of resistance: A sociolinguistic CDA of Biafra online discourses. *Discourse & Society, 23*(3), 217–244.

Christakos, L. T. G. (2015, September 2014). *By the numbers.* Retrieved from http://batterypark.ca/new-blog/2015/9/14/by-the-numbers

Christensen, L. T. G., & Cornelissen, J. (2011). Bridging corporate and organizational communication: Review, development and a look to the future. *Management Communication Quarterly, 25*(3).

Conrad, C. (1983). Organizational power: Faces and symbolic forms. In L. Putnam & M. Pacanowsky (Eds.), *Communication and organizations: An interpretive perspective* (pp. 173–194). London: Sage.

Coombs, W. T., & Holladay, S. J. (2008). Comparing apology to equivalent crisis response strategies: Clarifying apology's role and value in crisis communication. *Public Relations Review, 34*(3), 252–257.

Coleman, G. (2014). *Hacker, Hoaxer, whistleblower, Spy: The many faces of anonymous.* London: Verso.

Comas, J., Shrivastava, P., & Martin, E. C. (2015). Terrorism as formal organization, network, and social movement. *Journal of Management Inquiry, 24,* 47–60.

Coombs, W. T. (2007). Protecting organization reputations during a crisis: The development and application of situational crisis communication theory. *Corporate Reputation Review, 10*(3), 163–176.

Coombs, W. T., & Holladay, S. J. (2010). *PR strategy and application: Managing influence.* Hoboken, NJ: Wiley-Blackwell.

Cooren, F. (2004). Textual agency: How texts do things in organizational settings. *Organization, 11*(3), 373–393.

Cooren, F. (2010). *Action and agency in dialogue: Passion, incarnation and ventriloquism* (Vol. 6). Amsterdam, Netherlands: John Benjamins Publishing.

Cooren, F. (2012). Communication theory at the center: Ventriloquism and the communicative constitution of reality. *Journal of Communication, 62*(1), 1–20.

Cooren, F., & Fairhurst, G. (2009). Dislocation and stabilization: How to scale up from interactions to organization. In L. L. Putnam & A. M. Nicotera (Eds.), *Communication as constitutive of organizing* (pp. 117–152). Thousand Oaks, CA: Sage.

Cooren, F., Kuhn, T., Cornelissen, J. P., & Clark, T. (2011). Communication, organizing and organization: An overview and introduction to the special issue. *Organization Studies*, *32*(9), 1149–1170.

Cooren, F., & Taylor, J. R. (1997). Organization as an effect of mediation: Redefining the link between organization and communication. *Communication Theory*, *7*(219–259).

Corrigan, T. (2016, November 2). Social media activism: Effective or slacktivism? *Brand Driven Digital*. Retrieved October 2017, from www.branddrivendigital.com/social-media-activism-effective-slacktivism/

Cosgrove, C. (2011, December 22). The Brooklyn Warehouse gets bigger with help of friends. The Halifax *Chronicle Herald*.

Costanza-Chock, S., & Castells, M. (2014). *Out of the shadows, into the streets! Transmedia organizing and the immigrant rights movement*. Cambridge, MA: MIT press.

Crowdsourcing.org (2012). *Crowdfunding industry report*. Retrieved from http://www.crowdfunding.nl/wp-content/uploads/2012/05/92834651-Massolution-abridged-Crowd-Funding-Industry-Report1.pdf.

Currie, G., & Brown, A. D. (2003). A narratological approach to understanding processes of organizing in a UK hospital. *Human Relations*, *56*(5), 563–586.

Dawson, V. R. (2015). Who are we online? Changing perspectives toward organizational identity in social media context. *The Journal of Social Media in Society*, *4*(2).

Dean, J. (2012). *The communist horizon*. London: Verso.

Deetz, S. (1992). *Democracy in an age of corporate colonization: Developments in communication and the politics of everyday life*. Albany, NY: State University of New York Press.

Deetz, S., & Mumby, D. (1985). Metaphors, information, and power. In B. D. Ruben (Ed.), *Information and behavior* (Vol. 1, pp. 369–386). New Brunswick, NJ: Transaction Press.

Desanctis, G., & Poole, M. S. (1994). Capturing the complexity in advanced technology use – adaptive structuration theory. *Organization Science, 5*(2), 121–147.

Dobusch, L., & Schoeneborn, D. (2015). Fluidity, identity, and organizationality: The communicative constitution of Anonymous. *Journal of Management Studies*, *52*(8), 1005–1035.

Dowling, G. R. (1986). Managing your corporate images. *Industrial Marketing Management*, *15*(2), 109–115.

Dowling, J. B., MacDonald, V. N., & Protter, M. A. (1983). *The social realities of policing: Essays in legitimation theory*. Ottawa: Canadian Police College.

Drepper, T. (2005). *Organization and society: On the desideratum of a society theory of organizations in the work of Niklas Luhmann* (pp. 171–190). Malmö [etc.]: Liber, [Copenhagen]: Copenhagen Business School Press.

Druckman, J. N. (2001). The implications of framing effects for citizen competence. *Political Behavior*, *23*(3), 225–256.

Earl, J., Hunt, J., Garrett, R. K., & Dal, A. (2014). New technologies and social movements. In D. Della Porta & M. Diani (Eds.), *The oxford handbook of social movements*. Oxford: Oxford University Press. Advance online publication. Retrieved from http://www.oxfordhandbooks.com/view/10.1093/ oxfordhb/ 9780199678402.001.0001/oxfordhb-9780199678402-e-20

Emirbayer, M., & Mische, A. (1998). What is agency? *American Journal of Sociology*, *103*(4), 962–1023.

Entman, R. M. (1993). Framing: Toward clarification of a fractured paradigm. *Journal of Communication, 43*(4), 51–58.

Estellés-Arolas, E., & González-Ladrón-de-Guevara, F. (2012). Towards an integrated crowdsourcing definition. *Journal of Information science, 38*(2), 189–200.

Etter, M., Colleoni, E., Illia, L., Meggiorin, K., & D'Eugenio, A. (2017, December). Measuring organizational legitimacy in social media: Assessing citizens' judgement with sentiment analysis. *Business and Society,* 1–38.

Fairhurst, G. T. (2008). Discursive leadership: A communication alternative to leadership psychology. *Management Communication Quarterly, 21*(4), 510–521.

Fairhurst, G. T., & Putnam, L. L. (2004). Organizations as discursive constructions. *Communication Theory, 14,* 5–26.

Ferree, M. M., Gamson, W. A., Gerhards, J., & Rucht, D. (2002). *Shaping abortion discourse: Democracy and the public sphere in Germany and the United States.* New York, NY: Cambridge University Press.

Fiske, S. T., & Taylor, S. E. (1991). *Social cognition* (2nd ed.). New York, NY: McGraw-Hill.

Fiss, P. C., & Hirsch, P. M. (2005). The discourse of globalization: Framing and sensemaking of an emerging concept. *American Sociological Review, 70*(1), 29–52.

Flanagin, A. J., Stohl, C., & Bimber, B. (2006). Modeling the structure of collective action. *Communication Monographs, 73*(1), 29–54.

Flaxman, S., Goel, S., & Rao, J. M. (2016). Filter bubbles, echo chambers, and online news consumption. *Public Opinion Quarterly, 80*(S1), 298–320.

FoE Australia news. *Chain Reaction,* No. 121, 5–10. Retrieved August 2014, from https://search.informit.com.au/documentSummary;dn=439412544816738;res=IE LHSS. ISSN: 0312–1372.

Foucault, M. (1976). *1990: The history of sexuality, Vol 1: An introduction.* Trans. Robert Hurley. London: Penguin.

Fuchs, C. (2005). The mass media, politics, and warfare. In L. Artz & Y. Kamalipour (Eds.), *Bring 'Em on! media and politics in the Iraq war* (pp. 189–207). New York, NY: Rowman & Littlefield.

Gaden, G., & Dumitrica, D. (2014). The 'real deal': Strategic authenticity, politics and social media. *First Monday, 20*(1).

Gagliardi, P. (1986). The creation and change of organizational cultures: A conceptual framework. *Organization Studies, 7,* 117–134.

Garud, R., Jain, S., & Tuertscher, P. (2008). Incomplete by design and designing for incompleteness. *Organization Studies, 29,* 351–371.

Gephart, R. P., Jr. (1993). The textual approach: Risk and blame in disaster sensemaking. *Academy of Management Journal, 36*(6), 1465–1514.

Gephart, R. P., Topal, C., & Zhang, Z. (2010). Future-oriented sensemaking: Temporalities and institutional legitimation. In T. Hernes & S. Maitlis (Eds.), *Process, sensemaking, and organizing* (pp. 275–312). Oxford: Oxford University Press.

Gerbaudo, P. (2012). *Tweets and the streets.* London: Pluto Press.

Giddens, A. (1979). Agency, structure. In *Central problems in social theory* (pp. 49–95). London: Palgrave.

Giddens, A. (1984). *The constitution of society: Outline of the structuration theory.* Cambridge: Polity.

Gilpin, D. R., Palazzolo, E. T., & Brody, N. (2010). Socially mediated authenticity. *Journal of Communication Management, 14*(3), 258–278.

Gioia, D. A., Schultz, M., & Corley, K. G. (2000). Organizational identity, image, and adaptive instability. *Academy of Management Review*, 25(1), 63–81.

Gioia, D. A., & Thomas, J. (1996). Identity, image and issue interpretation: Sensemaking during strategic change in academia. *Administrative Science Quarterly*, 41(3), 370–403.

Gitlin, T. (1980). *The whole world is watching: Mass media in the making & unmaking of the new left*. Berkeley, CA: University of California Press.

Gladwell, M. (2010, October 4). Annals of innovation – small change – why the revolution will not be tweeted. *The New Yorker*. Retrieved March 4, 2013. https://www.newyorker.com/magazine/2010/10/04/small-change-malcolm-gladwell

Glozer, S., Caruana, R., & Hibbert, S. A. (2018). The never-ending story: Discursive legitimation in social media dialogue. *Organization Studies*, doi.org/10.11770170840617751006.

Goel, S., Hofman, J. M., & Irmak, S. M. (2012). *Who does what on the web: A large-scale study of browsing behavior*. Proceedings of the Sixth International AAAI Conference on Weblogs and Social Media, 1–8. ACM.

Goffman, E. (1959). *The presentation of self in everyday life*. Garden City, NY: Anchor Books/Doubleday.

Goffman, E. (1974). *Frame analysis: An essay on the organization of experience*. Cambridge, MA: Harvard University Press.

Grant, J. D., Keenoy, T. W., & Oswick, C. (Eds.). (1998). *Discourse and organization*. Thousand Oaks, CA: Sage.

Grant, J. D., & Mills, A. J. (2006). The quiet Americans: Formative context, the Academy of management leadership, and the management textbook, 1936–1960. *Management & Organizational History*, 1(2), 201–224.

Hall, E. T. (1983). *The dance of life: The other dimension of time*. New York, NY: Anchor Books/Doubleday.

Hammer, R. & Kellner, D. (2009). From communications and media studies through cultural studies. In R. Hammer & D. Kellner (Eds.), *Media/cultural studies: Critical approaches* (pp. ix–xlvii). New York, NY: Peter Lang.

Hardy, C. (2004). Scaling up and bearing down in discourse analysis: Questions regarding textual agencies and their context. *Organization*, 11(3), 415–425.

Hardy, C., & Phillips, N. (2004). Discourse and power. *The Sage handbook of organizational discourse*, 299, 316.

Hardy, C., & Phillips, N. (1999). No joking matter: Discursive struggle in the Canadian refugee system. *Organization Studies*, 20(1), 1–24.

Hartt, C. (2013). Actants without actors: Polydimensional discussion of a Regional Conference. *Tamara Journal of Critical Organisation Inquiry*, 11(3), 15.

Hartt, C. M., Mills, A. J., Mills, J. H., & Corrigan, L. T. (2014). Sense-making and actor networks: The non-corporeal actant and the making of an Air Canada history. *Management & Organizational History*, 9(3), 288–304.

Helms Mills, J. (2003). *Making sense of organizational change*. New York, NY: Routledge.

Helms Mills, J., & Mills, A. J. (2000). Rules, sensemaking, formative contexts, and discourse in the gendering of organizational culture. In N. Ashkanasy, C. Wilderom, & M. Peterson (Eds.), *Handbook of organizational culture and climate* (pp. 55–70). Thousand Oaks, CA/London/New Delhi: Sage.

Helms Mills, J., Thurlow, A., & Mills, A. J. (2010). Making sense of sensemaking: The critical sensemaking approach. *Qualitative Research in Organizations and Management: An International Journal*, 5(2), 182–195.

Herring, R. J. (2006). Why did "Operation Cremate Monsanto" fail? Science and class in India's great terminator-technology hoax. *Critical Asian Studies, 38*(4), 467–493.

Heverin, T., & Zach, L. (2012). Use of microblogging for collective sense-making during violent crises: A study of three campus shootings. *Journal of the Association for Information Science and Technology, 63*(1), 34–47.

Hockey, T. (2010). *The History.* Retrieved from http://www.hockeytheme.com/FrameRHistory.htm.

Hotten, R. (2015, December 10). Volkswagen: The scandal explained Business reporter. *BBC News.*

Howe, J. (2006a). The rise of crowdsourcing. *Wired Magazine, 14*(6), 1–4.

Howe, J. (2006b, June 2). Crowdsourcing: A definition. *Crowdsourcing: Why the power of the crowd is driving the future of business.* Weblog. Retrieved October 12, 2017, from http://crowdsourcing.typepad.com/cs/2006/06 /crowdsourcing_a.html

Howe, J. (2009). *Crowdsourcing: How the power of the crowd is driving the future of business.* New York, NY: Random House.

Humphreys, M., & Brown, A. D. (2002). Dress and identity: A Turkish case study. *Journal of Management Studies, 39*, 927–952.

Iyengar, S. (2005, November). Speaking of values: The framing of American politics. *The Forum, 3*(3). De Gruyter.

Jackson, D., Firtko, A., & Edenborough, M. (2007). Personal resilience as a strategy for surviving and thriving in the face of workplace adversity: A literature review. *Journal of Advanced Nursing, 60*(1), 1–9.

Jurgenson, N. (2012). When atoms meet bits: Social media, the mobile web and augmented revolution. *Future Internet, 4*(1), 83–91.

Juris, J. S. (2008). *Networking futures: The movements against corporate globalization.* Durham: Duke University Press.

Juris, J. S. (2012). Reflections on# occupy everywhere: Social media, public space, and emerging logics of aggregation. *American Ethnologist, 39*(2), 259–279.

Just, N., & Latzer, M. (2017). Governance by algorithms: Reality construction by algorithmic selection on the Internet. *Media, Culture & Society, 39*(2), 238–258.

Kahn, R., & Kellner, D. (2004). New media and internet activism: From the 'Battle of Seattle' to blogging. *New Media & Society, 6*(1), 87–95.

Kahneman, D. (2003). Maps of bounded rationality: A perspective on intuitive judgment and choice. In T. Fra¨ngsmyr (Ed.), *Les prix nobel: The nobel prizes* 2002 (pp. 449–489). Stockholm: Nobel Foundation.

Kahneman, D., & Egan, P. (2011). *Thinking, fast and slow* (Vol. 1). New York, NY: Farrar, Straus and Giroux.

Kane, G. C., Alavi, M., Labianca, G., & Borgatti, S. P. (2014). What's different about social media networks? A framework and research agenda. *MIS Quarterly, 38*(1), 275–304.

Kaplan, A. M., & Haenlein, M. (2010). Users of the world, unite! The challenges and opportunities of Social Media. *Business Horizons, 53*(1), 59–68.

Kavada, A. (2015). Creating the collective: Social media, the occupy movement and its constitution as a collective actor. *Information, Communication & Society, 18*(8), 872–886.

Kayes, D. C. (2004). The 1996 mount Everest climbing disaster: The breakdown of learning in teams. *Human Relations, 57*(10), 1263–1284.

Kent, M. L. (2008). Critical analysis of blogging in public relations. *Public Relations Review, 34*(1), 32–40.

Kent, M. L. (2013). Using social media dialogically: Public relations role in reviving democracy. *Public Relations Review, 39*(4), 337–345.

Kent, M. L., & Saffer, A. J. (2014). A Delphi study of the future of new technology research in public relations. *Public Relations Review, 40*(3), 568–576.

Kent, M. L., & Taylor, M. (2014). Problems with social media in public relations: Misremembering the past and ignoring the future. *International Journal of Interdisciplinary Research, 3*(2), 23–37.

Khang, H., Ki, E. J., & Ye, L. (2012). Social media research in advertising, communication, marketing, and public relations, 1997–2010. *Journalism & Mass Communication Quarterly, 89*(2), 279–298.

Khosravinik, M., & Unger, J. W. (2015). Critical discourse studies and social media: Power, resistance and critique in changing media ecologies. *Methods of Critical Discourse Studies*, 205–233.

Klein, G., Moon, B., & Hoffman, R. R. (2006). Making sense of sensemaking 1: Alternative perspectives. *IEEE Intelligent Systems, 21*(4), 70–73.

Koschmann, M. A. (2013). The communicative constitution of collective identity in interorganizational collaboration. *Management Communication Quarterly, 27*(1), 61–89.

Kravets, D. (2015, August 10 2:40p.m). VW says rogue engineers, not executives, responsible for emissions scandal. *Arts Technica*. Retrieved from https://arstechnica.com/tech-policy/2015/10/volkswagen-pulls-2016-diesel-lineup-from-us-market/

Kuhn, T. (2008). A communicative theory of the firm: Developing an alternative perspective on intra-organizational power and stakeholder relationships. *Organization Studies, 29*, 1227–1254.

Lammers, J. C. (2011). How institutions communicate: Institutional messages, institutional logics, and organisational communication. *Management Communication Quarterly, 25*(1), 154–182.

Latour, B. (2005). *Reassembling the social: An introduction to actor-network-theory*. Oxford: Oxford University Press.

Latour, B. (2013). *An inquiry into modes of existence*. Cambridge, MA: Harvard University Press.

Leclercq-Vandelannoitte, A. L. (2011). Organizations as discursive constructions: A Foucauldian approach. *Organization Studies, 32*(9).

Loader, B. D. (Ed.). (1997). *The governance of cyberspace: Politics, technology and global restructuring*. London, UK: Psychology Press.

Loader, B. D., & Mercea, D. (2011). Networking democracy? Social media innovations and participatory politics. *Information, Communication & Society, 14*(6), 757–769.

Lohr, J. (2015, October 20 Tuesday). Two thirds of Germans still trust Volkswagen. *The Guardian*. Retrieved from www.theguardian.com/business/2015/oct/20/two-thirds-of-germans-still-trust-volkswagen-after-emissions-scandal

Luhmann, N. (1992). What is communication? *Communication Theory, 2*, 251–259.

Luhmann, N. (1995). *Social systems*. Stanford: Stanford University Press.

Luhmann, N. (2003). Organization. In T. Bakken & T. Hernes (Eds.), *Autopoietic organization theory: Drawing on Niklas Luhmann's social systems perspective* (pp. 31–52). Oslo, Norway: Copenhagen Business School Press.

MacNamara, J., & Zerfass, A. (2012). Social media communication in organizations: The challenges of balancing openness, strategy, and management. *International Journal of Strategic Communication, 6*(4), 287–308.

Magala, S. J. (1997). Book review essay: Karl E. Weick: Sensemaking in organizations: 1995. *Organization Studies, 18*(2), 317–338. London: Sage. 231 pages.

Maitlis, S. (2005). The social processes of organizational sensemaking. *Academy of Management Journal, 48*(1), 21–49.

Maitlis, S., & Christianson, M. (2014). Sensemaking in organizations: Taking stock and moving forward. *The Academy of Management Annals, 8*(1), 57–125.

Maitlis, S., & Sonenshein, S. (2010). Sensemaking in crisis and change: Inspiration and insights from Weick (1988). *Journal of Management Studies, 47*(3), 551–580.

Majchrzak, A., Faraj, S., Kane, G. C., & Azad, B. (2013). The contradictory influence of social media affordances on online communal knowledge sharing. *Journal of Computer-Mediated Communication, 19*, 38–55.

March Against Monsanto (2015). Retrieved April 20, 2015, from https://www.march-against-monsanto.com/

Markus, H., & Zajonc, R. B. (1985). The cognitive perspective in social psychology. In G. Lindzey & E. Aronson (Eds.), *The handbook of social psychology: Special fields and applications* (Vol. 2, pp. 137–230). New York, NY: Random House.

Mason, P. (2013). *Why it's still kicking off everywhere: The new global revolutions.* Verso.

Mattoni, A., & Treré, E. (2014). Media practices, mediation processes, and mediatization in the study of social movements. *Communication Theory, 24*(3), 252–271.

McPhee, R. D. (1998). Giddens' conception of personal relationships and its relevance to communication theory. In R. Conville & E. Rogers (Eds.), *The meaning of "relationship" in interpersonal communication* (pp. 83–106). Westport, CT: Praeger.

McPhee, R. D., & Iverson, J. (2009). Agents of constitution in Communidad: Constitutive processes of communication in organizations. In L. L. Putnam & A. M. Nicotera (Eds.), *Building theories of organization: The constitutive role of communication* (pp. 49–87). New York, NY: Routledge.

McPhee, R. D., & Zaug, P. (2000). The communicative constitution of organizations: A framework for explanation. *Electronic Journal of Communication/La Revue Electronique de Communication, 10*(1/2), 1–16.

McPhee, R. D., & Zaug, P. (2009). The communicative constitution of organizations. *Building theories of organization: The constitutive role of communication, 10*(1–2), 21.

Merli, A. (2015). Caso Volkswagen, Wolfsburg Studia I Social per Limitare I Danni. *Il Sole 24 ORE.*

Messing, S., & Westwood, S. J. (2012). *How social media introduces biases in selecting and processing news content.* Working paper, Retrieved from http://www.stanford.edu/seanjw/papers/SMH.pdf

Meyer, N. (2013, December 24). *Interview with Tami Canal, March against Monsanto founder.* Retrieved from https://fatvox.com/interview-with-tami-canal-march-against-monsanto-founder/

Miller, K. (2004). *Communication theories: Perspectives, processes and contexts.* New York, NY: McGraw-Hill.

Mills, A. J., & Murgatroyd, S. J. (1991). *Organization rules.* Milton Keynes: Open University Press.

Mills, J. H., & Weatherbee, T. G. (2006). Hurricanes hardly happen: Sensemaking as a framework for understanding organizational disasters. *Culture and Organization, 12*(3), 265–279.

Minsky, M. (1975, June). *Minsky's frame system theory.* In TINLAP'75: Proceedings of the 1975 workshop on Theoretical issues in natural language processing (pp. 104–116).

Morozov, E. (2009, May 19). The brave new world of slacktivism. *Foreign Policy* (blog). Retrieved from http://neteffect.foreignpolicy.com/posts/2009/05/19/the_brave_new_world_of_slacktivism

Mumby, D. K. (1987). The political function of narrative in organizations. *Communication Monographs, 54,* 113–127. doi:10.1080/03637758709390221

Mumby, D. K., & Stohl, C. (1991). Power and discourse in organization studies: Absence and the dialectic of control. *Discourse & Society, 2,* 313–332. doi: 10.1177/0957926591002003004

Munro, I., & Huber, C. (2012). Kafka's mythology: Organization, bureaucracy and the limits of sensemaking. *Human Relations, 65*(4), 523–543.

Navis, C., & Glynn, M. A. (2011). Legitimate distinctiveness and the entrepreneurial identity: Influence on investor judgments of new venture plausibility. *Academy of Management Review, 36*(3), 479–499.

Nelson, T. E., Oxley, Z. M., & Clawson, R. A. (1997). Toward a psychology of framing effects. *Political Behavior, 19*(3), 221–246.

Obendorf, H. W., Herder Eelco, H., & Matthias, M. (2007). *Web page revisitation revisited: implications of a long-term click-stream study of browser usage.* Proceedings of the SIGCHI Conference on Human Factors in Computing Systems, 597–606. ACM.

O'Mahony, S., & Ferraro, F. (2007). The emergence of governance in an open source community. *Academy of Management Journal, 50,* 1079–1106.

Oram, A. (2009). *What sociologist Erving Goffman could tell us about social networking and internet identity.* Retrieved from http://radar.oreilly.com/2009/10/what-sociologist-erving-goffma.html

Orlikowski, W. J. (1992). The duality of technology: Rethinking the concept of technology in organizations. *Organization Science, 3*(3), 398–427.

Oswick, C., Grant, D., Michelson, G., & Wailes, N. (2005). Looking forwards: Discursive directions in organizational change. *Journal of Organizational Change Management, 18*(4), 383–390.

Paget, M. A. 1988. *The Unity of Mistakes.* Philadelphia, PA: Temple University Press.

Painter, C., & Martins, J. T. (2017). Organisational communication management during the Volkswagen diesel emissions scandal: A hermeneutic study in attribution, crisis management, and information orientation. *Knowledge and Process Management, 24*(3), 204–218.

Pariser, E. (2011). *The filter bubble: How the new personalized web is changing what we read and how we think.* London, UK: Penguin.

Parker, S. (2015, October 30). The implosion of a brand: A Twitter timeline of the Volkswagen emissions scandal. *Union Metrics.* Retrieved from https://unionmetrics.com/blog/2015/10/implosion Brand-twitter-timeline-volkswagen-emissions-scandal/

Patriotta, G. (2003). Sensemaking on the shop floor: Narratives of knowledge in organizations. *Journal of Management Studies, 40*(2), 349–375.

Patriotta, G., & Brown, A. D. (2011). Sensemaking, metaphors and performance evaluation. *Scandinavian Journal of Management, 27*(1), 34–43.

Patriotta, G., Gond, J. P., & Schultz, F. (2011). Maintaining legitimacy: Controversies, orders of worth, and public justifications. *Journal of Management Studies, 48*(8), 1804–1836.

Pearson, C. M., & Clair, J. A. (1998). Reframing crisis management. *Academy of Management Review, 23*(1), 59–76.

Pemmaraju, N., Mesa, R. A., Majhail, N. S., & Thompson, M. A. (2017, October). The use and impact of Twitter at medical conferences: Best practices and Twitter etiquette. *Seminars in Hematology, 54*(4), 184–188. Elsevier.

Pepsodent. (1950, 18 September). Pepsodent's "My friend Irma" $100 000 Contest, *Life*, 5.

Perry, D. C., Taylor, M., & Doerfel, M. L. (2003). Internet-based communication in crisis management. *Management Communication Quarterly, 17*(2), 206–232.

Pfeffer, J., & Davis-Blake, A. (1987). Understanding organizational wage structures: A resource dependence approach. *Academy of Management Journal, 30*, 437–455.

Pfeffer, J., & Salancik, G. R. (1974). Organizational decision making as a political process: The case of a university budget. *Administrative Science Quarterly, 19*, 135–151.

Phillips, N., & Hardy, C. (2002). *Discourse analysis: Investigating processes of social construction*. Thousand Oaks, CA: Sage.

Pinchevski, A. (2005). *By way of interruption: Levinas and the ethics of communication*. Pittsburgh, PA: Duquesne University Press.

Polkinghorne, D. E. (1998). Narrative Psychologie und Geschichtsbewußtsein. *Beziehungen und Perspektiven.* na.

Postill, J. (2013). Democracy in an age of viral reality: A media epidemiography of Spain's indignados movement. *Ethnography, 15*(1), 51–69.

Postman, N. (1993). *Technopoly: The surrender of culture to technology*. New York, NY: Vintage Books.

Poyntz, N. (2011). *Seventeenth-century crowd funding*. Retrieved January 7, 2018, from https://mercuriuspoliticus.wordpress.com/2011/12/13/seventeenth-century-crowd-funding/

Puranam, P., Alexy, O., & Reitzig, M. (2014). What's "new" about new forms of organizing? *Academy of Management Review, 39*(2), 162–180.

Purser, R. E., & Petranker, J. (2005). Unfreezing the future: Exploring the dynamic of time in organizational change. *The Journal of Applied Behavioral Science, 41*(2), 182–203.

Putnam, L. L. (2005). Discourse analysis: Mucking around with negotiation data. *International Negotiation, 10*(1), 17–32.

Putnam, L. L., & Cooren, F. (2004). Alternative perspectives on the role of text and agency in constituting organizations. *Organization, 11*(3), 323–333.

Putnam, L. L., & Fairhurst, G. T. (2015). Revisiting "organizations as discursive constructions": 10 years later. *Communication Theory, 25*(4), 375–392.

Putnam, L. L., & McPhee, R. D. (2008). Theory building: Comparisons of CCO orientations. In *Building theories of organization: The constitutive role of communication*. Abingdon: Routledge Taylor & Francis Group.

Putnam, L. L., & Nicotera, A. M. (Eds.). (2009). *Building theories of organization: The constitutive role of communication*. London: Routledge.

Putnam, L. L., & Nicotera, A. M. (2010). Communicative constitution of organization is a question: Critical issues for addressing it. *Management Communication Quarterly*, 24(1).

Puzzanghera, J., & Hirsch, J. (2015). VW Hearing. *Los Angeles Times*, Retrieved October 8, 2015, from www.latimes.com/business/autos/la-fi-hy-vw-hearing-20151009-story.html

Qaim, M. (2016). The complex public debate. In *Genetically modified crops and agricultural development* (pp. 135–163). New York, NY: Palgrave Macmillan.

Qiu, C. (2013) *Issues in crowdfunding: Theoretical and empirical investigation on Kickstarter, SSRN*. Retrieved October 27, 2013, from https://ssrn.com/abstract=2345872 or http://dx.doi.org/10.2139/ssrn.2345872

Rainie, L., & Smith, A. (2012). *Social networking sites and politics*. Washington, DC: Pew Internet & American Life Project. Retrieved June 12, 2012, from http://www.pewinternet.org/2012/03/12/social-networking-sites-and-politics/

Reisigl, M., & Wodak, R. (2001). *Discourse and discrimination*. London: Routledge.

Rheingold, H. (2002), 'Mobile Virtual Communities', *Receiver*, 6, 1–4. Retrieved August 18, 2010, from http://www. vodafone.com/flash/receiver/06/articles/pdf/02.pdf.

Rhodes, C. (2001). *Writing organization: (Re)presentation and control in narratives at work* (Vol. 7). Amsterdam, Netherlands: John Benjamins Publishing.

Rouse, J. (2005). Power/Knowledge. In G. Gutting (Ed.), *The Cambridge companion to Foucault* (Cambridge Companions to Philosophy, pp. 95–122). Cambridge: Cambridge University Press. doi:10.1017/CCOL0521840821.005

Ruel, S. (2018). *Multiplicity of "I's" in intersectionality: Women's exclusion from STEM management in the Canadian space industry*. Doctoral Dissertation – Athabasca University. http://hdl.handle.net/10791/254

Rumelhart, D. E. (1984). Schemata and the cognitive system. In J. R. S. Wyer & T. K. Srull (Eds.), *Handbook of social cognition* (Vol. 1, pp. 161–188). Hillsdale, NJ: Erlbaum.

Salancik, G. R. and Pfeffer, J. (1978). A social information processing approach to job attitude and task design. *Administrative Science Quarterly*, 23, 224–53.

Sánchez, J. L. (2011, May 26). Los primeros 40 de Sol. *Periodismo Humano*. Retrieved from http://periodismohumano.com/temas-destacados/los-primeros-40-de-sol.html

Seidl, D. (2007). General strategy concepts and the ecology of strategy discourses: A systemic-discursive perspective. *Organization Studies*, 28(2), 197–218.

Schank, R. C., & Abelson, R. P. (1977). *Scripts, plans, goals and understanding: An inquiry into human knowledge structures*. Hillsdale, NJ: Erlbaum.

Schoeneborn, D., Blaschke, S., Cooren, F., McPhee, R. D., Seidl, D., & Taylor, J. R. (2014). The three schools of CCO thinking: Interactive dialogue and systematic comparison. *Management Communication Quarterly*, 28(2), 285–316.

Schoeneborn, D., & Scherer, A. G. (2012). 'Clandestine organizations, al Qaeda, and the para dox of (in)visibility: A response to Stohl and Stohl'. *Organization Studies*, 33, 963–971.

Schoeneborn, D., & Trittin, H. (2013). Transcending transmission: Towards a constitutive perspective on CSR communication. *Corporate Communications: An International Journal*, 18(2), 193–211.

Schoeneborn, D., & Vasquez, C. (2017). Communicative constitution of organizations. *International Encyclopedia of Organizational Communication*, 367–386. http://doi.org/10.1002/9781118955567.wbieoc030

Schreyogg, G., & Sydow, J. (2010). 'Organizing for fluidity? Dilemmas of new organizational forms'. *Organization Science, 21*, 1251–1262.

Schultz, F., Castelló, I., & Morsing, M. (2013). The construction of corporate social responsibility in network societies: A communication view. *Journal of Business Ethics, 115*(4), 681–692.

Scott, C. (2013). *Anonymous agencies, backstreet businesses, and covert collectives: Rethinking organizations in the 21st century.* Stanford, CA: Stanford University Press.

Schenk, E., & Guittard, C. (2011). Towards a characterization of crowdsourcing practices. *Journal of Innovation Economics & Management, 7*(1), 93–107.

Schenk, E., & Guittard, C. (2009, December). Crowdsourcing: What can be outsourced to the crowd, and why. In *Workshop on open source innovation, Strasbourg, France* (Vol. 72, p. 3).

Scott, W. R. (2004). Reflections on a half-century of organizational sociology. *Annual Review of Sociology, 30*, 1–21. doi:10.1146/annurev.soc.30.012703.110644

Seidl, D. & Becker, K. H. (2006). Organisations as distinction generating and processing systems: Niklas Luhmann's contribution to organisation studies. *Organization, 13*(1), 9–35.

Sergi, V., & Bonneau, C. (2016). Making mundane work visible on social media: A CCO investigation of working out loud on Twitter. *Communication Research and Practice, 2*(3), 378–406.

Shirky, C. (2011). The political power of social media: Technology, the public sphere, and political change. *Foreign Affairs*, 28–41.

Shrivastava, P., Mitroff, I. I., Miller, D., & Miclani, A. (1988). Understanding industrial crises [1]. *Journal of Management Studies, 25*(4), 285–303.

Sillince, J. A. (2010). Can CCO theory tell us how organizing is distinct from markets, networking, belonging to a community, or supporting a social movement? *Management Communication Quarterly, 24*(1), 132–138.

Social media reaction to the VW emission scandal. Retrieved from www.mediameasurement.com/uncategorized/social-medias-reaction-vw-emissions-scandal/

Sniderman, P., & Theriault, S. (2004). The structure of political argument and the logic of issue framing. In W. E. Saris & P. Sniderman (Eds.), *Studies in public opinion: Attitudes nonattitudes, measurement error and change.* Princeton, NJ: Princeton University Press.

Spijkers, O. (2016). The world's citizens get involved in global policymaking: Global resistance, global public participation, and global democracy. *Inter Gentes: McGill Journal of International Law & Legal Pluralism, 1*(1), 18–29.

Stieglitz, S., Mirbabaie, M., & Potthoff, T. (2018, January). *Crisis communication on Twitter during a global crisis of Volkswagen-the case of "Dieselgate".* In Proceedings of the 51st Hawaii International Conference on System Sciences.

Stigliani, I., & Ravasi, D. (2012). Organizing thoughts and connecting brains: Material practices and the transition from individual to group-level prospective sensemaking. *Academy of Management Journal, 55*(5), 1232–1259.

Stohl, C., & Stohl, M. (2011). Secret agencies: The communicative constitution of a clandestine organization. *Organization Studies, 32*, 1197–1215.

Sunstein, C. R. (2018). *# Republic: Divided democracy in the age of social media.* Princeton, NJ: Princeton University Press.

Suchman, M. C. (1995). Managing legitimacy: Strategic and institutional approaches. *Academy of Management Review, 20*(3), 571–610.

Suddaby, R. (2011). How communication institutionalizes: A response to Lammers. *Management Communication Quarterly, 25*, 183–190.

Suddaby, R., Bitektine, A., & Haack, P. (2017). Legitimacy. *Academy of Management Annals, 11*(1), 451–478.

Suddaby, R., & Greenwood, R. (2005). Rhetorical strategies of legitimacy. *Administrative Science Quarterly, 50*, 35–67.

Sutcliffe, K. M. (2013). Sensemaking. In M. Augier & D. Teece (Eds.), *The Palgrave encyclopedia of strategic management*. Basingstoke: Palgrave Macmillan.

Sweetser, E., & Fauconnier, G. (1996). Cognitive links and domains: Basic aspects of mental space theory. *Spaces, Worlds, and Grammar, 1228*.

Taylor, J.R. (1999) What is "organizational communication"? Communication as a dialogic of text and conversation, *The Communication Review*, 3: 1–2, 21–63, DOI: 10.1080/10714429909368573

Taylor, J. R. (2009). Organizing from the bottom up? Reflections on the constitution of organization in communication. In L. L. Putnam & A. M. Nicotera (Eds.), *Building theories of organization: The constitutive role of communication* (pp. 153–186). London: Routledge.

Taylor, J. R., & Cooren, F. (1997). What makes communication 'organizational'? How the many voices of a collectivity become the one voice of an organization. *Journal of Pragmatics, 27*(4), 409–438.

Taylor, J. R., & Van Every, E. J. (2000) *The emergent organization: communication, its site and surface*. Mahwah, NJ: Lawrence Erlbaum Associates.

Taylor, J. R., & Van Every, E. J. (2011). *The situated organization: Case Sstudies in the pragmatics of communication research* New York: Routledge.

Taylor, J. R., Cooren, F., Giroux, H., & Robichaud, D. (1996). The communicational basis of organization: Between the conversation and the text. *Communication Theory, 6*(1), 1–39.

Taylor, M., & Kent, M. L. (2010). Anticipatory socialization in the use of social media in public relations: A content analysis of PRSA's Public Relations Tactics. *Public Relations Review, 36*(3), 207–214.

Taylor, M., & Perry, D. C. (2005). Diffusion of traditional and new media tactics in crisis communication. *Public Relations Review, 31*(2), 209–217.

Tewksbury, D., & Scheufele, D. A. (2007). Special issue on framing, agenda setting, and priming: Agendas for theory and research. *Journal of Communication, 57*(1), 8–8.

Thorhauge, A. M. (2012). Communication technologies in the study environment: Institutional and personal media as a reflection of organisational structure. *MedieKultur: Journal of Media and Communication Research, 28*(53), 15.

Thurlow, A. (2010). Critical sensemaking. *Sage Encyclopedia of Case Study Research, 1*, 257–260.

Thurlow, A. (2007). *Meaningful change: Making sense of the discourse of the language of change*. (Doctoral Dissertation) Saint Mary's University, Halifax Canada. Retrieved August 18, 2018 from: http://library2.smu.ca/xmlui/bitstream/handle/01/9026/thurlow_amy_phd_2007.PDF;sequence=2

Thurlow, A., & Helms Mills, J. (2009). Change, talk and sensemaking. *Journal of Organizational Change Management, 22*(5), 459–479.

Thurlow, A., & Yue, A. R. (2013). *Out with the in Crowd: Constructing the individual in a crowdsourcing environment*. Workplace Review, October 2013 Issue, 44–52.

Treem, J. W., & Leonardi, P. M. (2013). Social media use in organisations: Exploring the affordances of visibility, editability, persistence, and association, *Annals of the International Communication Association, 36*(1), 143–189.

Treleaven, L., & Sykes, C. (2005). Loss of organizational knowledge: From supporting clients to serving head office. *Journal of Organizational Change Management*, *18*(4), 353–368.

Townley, B. (1994). *Reframing human resource management: Power, ethics and the subject at work*. London: Sage.

Tambini, D., Bryan, C., & Tsagarousianou, R. (Eds.) (1998). *Cyberdemocracy: Technology, cities and civic networks*. London: Routledge.

Tsoukas, H., & Chia, R. (2002). On organizational becoming: Rethinking organizational change. *Organization Science*, *13*(5), 567–582.

Turkle, S. (1995). *Life on the screen: Identity in the age of the internet*. New York, NY: Simon & Schuster.

Turkle, S. (2011). *Alone together: Why we expect more from technology and less from ourselves*. New York, NY: Basic Books.

Turner, B. A. (1976). The organizational and interorganizational development of disaster. *Administrative Science Quarterly*, *21*, 378–397.

Twitterstorm. (2018, January 3). Retrieved from https://www.techopedia.com/definition/29624/twitterstorm

Unger, J., Wodak, R., & Khosravinik, M. (2016). Critical discourse studies and social media data. *Qualitative Research*, 227–293.

Unger, R. M. (1987). *False necessity: Anti-necessitarian social theory in the service of radical democracy*. CUP Archive.

Upton, J. (2013, May 27). As world marches against Monsanto, Senators protect it from labeling laws. *Grist*. Retrieved from http://grist.org/food/as-world-marches-against-monsanto- senators-protect-it-from-labeling-laws/

Vaara, E., & Tienari, J. (2008). A discursive perspective on legitimation strategies in multinational corporations. *Academy of Management Review*, *33*(4), 985–993.

Vaara, E., Tienari, J., & Laurila, J. (2006). Pulp and paper fiction: On the discursive legitimation of global industrial restructuring. *Organization Studies*, *27*(6), 789–813.

Vallee, J. (1982). *The network revolution: Confessions of a computer scientist*. Berkeley, CA: And/Or Press.

Van Dijk, T. A. (1993). Principles of critical discourse analysis. *Discourse and Society*, *4*(2), 249–283.

Van Leeuwen, T., & Wodak, R. (1999). Legitimizing immigration control: A discourse-historical analysis. *Discourse Studies*, *1*(1), 83–118.

Vendelo, M. T., & Rerup, C. (2009, August). *Weak cues and attentional triangulation: The Pearl Jam concert accident at Roskilde Festival*. In Academy of Management Annual Meeting. Chicago, IL. VW study netlytics. Retrieved from https://dieselgatescandal.wordpress.com/2017/01/22/data-scrapping-with-netlytic-and-data-visualization-with-gephi/

Weber, K., & Glynn, M. A. (2006). Making sense with institutions: Context, thought and action in Karl Weick's theory. *Organization Studies*, *27*(11), 1639–1660.

Weick, K. (1969). *The social psychology of organizing*. Reading, MA: Addison-Wesley,

Weick, K. E. (1979). *The social psychology of organizing* (2nd ed.). Reading, MA: Addison- Wesley.

Weick, K. E. (1988). Enacted sensemaking in crisis situations [1]. *Journal of Management Studies*, *25*(4), 305–317.

Weick, K. E. (1990). The vulnerable system: An analysis of the Tenerife air disaster. *Journal of Management*, *16*, 571–93.

Weick, K. E. (1993). The collapse of sensemaking: The Mann Gulch disaster. *Administrative Science Quarterly, 38*, 628–652.

Weick, K. E. (1995). Sensemaking in organizations. Thousand Oaks, CA: Sage Publications.

Weick, K. E. (1996). Enactment and the boundaryless career: Organizing as we work. The Boundaryless Career: A New Employment Principle for a New Organizational Era, 40–57.

Weick, K. E. (2003). Positive organizing and organizational tragedy. *Positive Organizational Scholarship: Foundations of a New Discipline*, 66–80.

Weick, K. E. (2010). Reflections on enacted sensemaking in the Bhopal disaster. *Journal of Management Studies, 47*(3), 537–550.

Weick, K. E., Gilfillan, D. P., & Keith, T. (1973). The effect of composer credibility on orchestra performance. *Sociometry, 36*, 435–462.

Weick, K. E., & Sutcliffe, K. M. (2003). Hospitals as cultures of entrapment: a reanalysis of the Bristol Royal Infirmary. *California Management Review, 45*, 73–84.

Weick, K. E., Sutcliffe, K., & Obstfeld, D. (2005). Organizing and the process of sensemaking. *Organization Science, 16*(4), 409–421.

Westwood, R., & Clegg, S. (Eds.). (2009). *Debating organization: Point-counterpoint in organization studies*. Hoboken, NJ: John Wiley & Sons.

Wiebe, E. (2010). Temporal sensemaking: Managers' use of time to frame organizational change. In T. Hernes & S. Maitlis (Eds.), *Process, sensemaking, & organizing* (pp. 213–241). Oxford: Oxford University Press.

Wicks, R. H. (1992). Schema theory and measurement in mass communication research: Theoretical and methodological issues in news information processing. *Communication Yearbook, 15*, 115–145.

Wicks, D. (2002). Institutionalized mindsets of invulnerability: Differentiated institutional fields and the antecedents of organizational crisis. *Organization Studies, 22*, 659–692.

Wilson Quarterly. (2011, Spring). Tweeting toward freedom? *Wilsonquarterly.com.* Retrieved from www.wilsonquarterly.com/article.cfm?AID=1828

Wodak, R., & Fairclough, N. (2010). Recontextualizing European higher education policies: The cases of Austria and Romania. *Critical Discourse Studies, 7*(1), 19–40. doi:10.1080/17405900903453922

Zhao, D., & Rosson, M. B. (2009, May). How and why people Twitter: The role that micro-blogging plays in informal communication at work. In *Proceedings of the ACM 2009 international conference on supporting group work* (pp. 243–252). United States: ACM Association for Computing Machinery.

Zijderveld, A. C. (1970). Rationality and irrationality in pluralistic society. *Social Research*, 23–47.

Zilber, T. B. (2007). Stories and the discursive dynamics of institutional entrepreneurship: The case of Israeli high-tech after the Bubble. *Organisation Studies, 28*(7), 1035–1054.

Index

Note: Page numbers in *italic* indicate figures.

Actor Network Theory (ANT) 13–14, 31, 75–76, 110
Adam, B. 106
agency: collective enactment of meaning and 46; communication as constitutive of organization (CCO) theory and 20, 22, 48; Critical Sensemaking (CSM) framework and 40, 48; cue selection process and 100; future work on question of 110; identifying sites of 76–77; non-human 14; power and 19; reconceptualization of human 106; relationship between the individual and 48; sensemaking and 28, 32, 108; sharing of 45; textual 15, 16, 17
Alavi, M. 3
Albu, O. B. 2
Alone Together 20
Appbacker 58
authenticity 43–45, 70, 105
authorization 67
authorizing, discursive 69
Awesome Foundation 62–65

Bannerman, S. 58
Barger, J. 44
Barros, M. 88–89, 94
Bateson, G. 25
Becker, K. H. 47
Benkler, Y. 56
Bennett, S. 88, 89, 90, 96
Bignell, L. 103
Bimber, B. 85
Bisel, R. S. 10, 20, 108
Blackler, F. 70
Blaschke, S. 47–48

blogging 36, 44
Boje, D. M. 30
Bonneau, C. 45
Borgatti, S. P. 3
Boyd, D. M. 3, 19
bracketing 74–75
Brooklyn Warehouse 59–62
Brown, S. D. 93
Brummans, B. H. J. M. 11–12

Cacciatore, M. A. 50, 51, 53
Capella, J. 50
Caruana, R. 68–69
chats, online 36
Chia, R. 15
Chiluwa, I. 96
Christakos, L. 60, 62
Christianson, M. 24, 26–30
Claman, D. 58
Clark, T. 4
Clawson, R. A. 52–53
collaboration 16, 49–50, 53, 109
collective enactment 46, 86
communication as constitutive of organization (CCO) theory 3–5, 22, 107–108; central focus in 8–9; connection between micro-level and macro-level production 47–49; fluid organizations and 15–16; Four Flows approach in 10–11, 18, 65, 73, 107; human and non-human actants in 75; Luhmann's Theory of Social Systems in 11–12, 14; methodology in (*see* discourse analysis methodology); Montreal School of organizational communication and 9–10, 12–17, 45, 107; order and disorder and 72–73; range of methodologies in 8

Coombs, W. T. 84

Cooren, F. 2, 4, 11–12, 14–19, 18, 38, 45, 72, 76

Cornelissen, J. P. 4

crises, organizational 73–74, 77; *see also* Volkswagen

critical discourse analysis 38

Critical Sensemaking (CSM) framework 4–5, 13–14, 108; Actor Network Theory combined with 31, 75–76; formative contexts in 31–32, 70–71; framing and 51–52; human and non-human actants in 75–76; legitimation and 68; methodology in (*see* discourse analysis methodology); order and disorder and 72; purpose of 22; text analysis in 41; *see also* sensemaking

crowdfunding/crowdsourcing 57–58, 109; popular platforms for 58–59; social action and 59–65

cues in sensemaking 25–26, 39, 55–56, 100

cyberlibertarians 87

Dean, J. 88

Delphi technique 49, 71

democratization through social media 49–50

Dewey, J. 13

#dieselgate *see* Volkswagen

digital democracy 87

discourse analysis methodology 40; context of text and 37–38; discourse analysis 40; disputing your own interpretation and explanation in 42; examining communication actions and transactions in 38–39; looking for inconsistencies, ironies or unexpected occurrences 42; mapping information flow in 37; text and context in 41; web based tools in 36; working back and forth between text and concepts in 41–42

discourse of resistance 96

discursive approach to sensemaking 30, 67

discursive authorizing 69

discursive finalization 69

discursive resistance 94–95, 96

discursive validation 69

Dobusch, L. 15–16

Doerfel, M. L. 73

dominant reading 19

Druckman, J. N. 50, 52

Dumitrica, D. 43–44

EdgeRank 54

Eli Lilly company 57

Ellison, N. B. 3, 19

Emirbayer, M. 106

emphasis framing 52–53

enactment 26–27, 39–40, 44–45, 91–92; collective 46, 86; editability of sensemaking enhancing 94; of meaning, collective 46; plausibility and 45–49; power and 92; in public spaces versus virtual public spaces 86; social activism and 85–86

engagement, rules of 101–102

Entman, R. M. 51, 52–53

Environmental Protection Agency (EPA) 79, 80, 84

environment and sensemaking 26–27, 39–40

equivalency framing 51

Etter, M. 2

Facebook 36, 49, 54, 98–99

Fairclough, N. 90

Fairhurst, G. T. 10, 13, 107

Fauconnier, G. 50

filter bubbles 54

finalization, discursive 69

Fiss, P. C. 56

Flanagin, A. J. 85

Flaxman, S. 56

Flickr 19

formative contexts in CSM 31–32

forums, online 36

Foucault, M. 3, 33, 76, 91, 94

Four Flows approach 10–11, 18, 65, 73, 107

fragmentation 49–50, 108–109

Framing Theory 13, 50–56, 110

Gaden, G. 43–44

Gagliardi, P. 1

Gephart, R. P. 29

Gerbaudo, P. 65, 87

Giddens, A. 11

Gioia, D. A. 1, 24

Gitlin, T. 51

Gladwell, M. 87

globalization from below 59, 110

Glozer, S. 68–69

Glynn, M. A. 25, 66
Goel, S. 56
Goffman, E. 51
GoFundMe 58
Google analytics 36
Guittard, C. 57

Hacksimov, I. 86
Haenlein, M. 3, 104
Hall, E. T. 106
Hammer, R. 59
Hardy, C. 40, 89
Hartt, C. 31, 75–76
Helms Mills, J. 23–24, 29, 30–34, 39,
    51, 90, 91–92
Heverin, T. 75
Hibbert, S. A. 68–69
Hirsch, J. 82
Hirsch, P. M. 56
Hoffman, R. R. 23
Holladay, S. J. 84
Hootsuite 36
Howe, J. 57, 58
Huber, C. 67
human and non-human actants
    75–77
hyper-intertextuality 88–90
hyper-recontextualization 90

identity construction: authenticity in
    44; contest nature of 30; sensemaking
    and 24–26,
    33–34
ideological segregation 56
Indiegogo 58
Indignados movement 85–86
individual sensemaking 91–92
InnoCentive project 57
Instagram 36
Internet Relay Chat (IRC) 80
intertextuality 88–89
Iverson, J. 65

James, W. 13
Jamieson, K. H. 50
Juris, J. S. 85
Just, N. 71

Kahn, R. 59, 109
Kahneman, D. 51
Kane, G. C. 3
Kaplan, A. M. 3, 104
Kavada, A. 48

Kellner, D. 59, 109
Kent, M. L. 49, 53, 55, 70–71, 77,
    108–109
Khosravinik, M. 2, 37–38
Kickstarter 58–59
Kiva 59
Klein, G. 23
Klout 36
Koschmann, M. A. 4, 9, 16–18
Kuhn, T. 4, 18–19

Labianca, G. 3
Latzer, M. 71
Laurila, J. 88
Leclercq-Vandelannoitte, A. L. 3, 95
legitimation 43, 66–69, 100, 105;
    five categories of 67; forms of 69;
    fragmentation and 49–50
Leonardi, P. M. 92
Life magazine 58
Lightfoot, G. 93
Loader, B. D. 86
Luhmann's Theory of Social Systems
    11–12, 14

MacNamara, J. 5
Maitlis, S. 24, 26–30, 51, 73–75
#MarchAgainstMonsanto *see*
    Monsanto
McPhee, R. 9–11, 10–11, 22, 64, 65,
    102
Mercea, D. 86
Messina, C. 80
Messing, S. 54–55
micro-blogging 45
micro- versus macro-level
    communication contexts 47–49
Miller, K. 32, 91
Mills, A. J. 26, 29, 32, 90
Minsky, M. 53
Mische, A. 106
Monsanto 96–97, 107; legitimation
    and 100; local and offline organizing
    against 103; organizational identity
    of 98; rules of engagement and
    101–102; sensemaking and 99–100;
    Tami Canal and 98–99; Twitterstorm
    against 100–102
Montreal School of organizational
    communication 9–10, 12–17, 45,
    107
Moon, B. 23
moralization 67

Munro, I. 67
Murgatroyd, S. J. 32

narrative storytelling 30; enacted
    sensemaking and 45–49
narrativization 67
Navis, C. 66
Nelson, T. E. 52–53
Netlytic 36, 65, 102
network of meanings 18–19
Nicotera, A. M. 4, 8–9, 11, 17, 102
normalization 67
noticing 74–75

Obstfeld, D. 1–2
ongoing process, sensemaking as 27,
    93–94
online communities 36
Oram, A. 70
order and disorder 71–75
organizational crises 73–74, 77; *see
    also* Volkswagen
organizational identity 1–6; CCO
    perspectives and (*see* communication
    as constitutive of organization
    (CCO) theory); Critical Sensemaking
    and (*see* Critical Sensemaking
    (CSM) framework); fluid forms of
    15; methodology in studying (*see*
    discourse analysis methodology);
    micro-level 28; rules theory and 33,
    39–40
Orlikowski, W. 18
Oxley, Z. M. 52–53

Pariser, E. 54
Parnell, M. 103
Peirce, C. S. 13
Pepsodent brand 58
perception as reference dependent
    51–52
Perry, D. C. 73
Phillips, N. 40
plausibility 26, 30, 33–34, 105;
    authenticity and 43–45, 70; enacted
    sensemaking and 45–49; formative
    context in 70–71; intersection
    between sensemaking and 66–69
plausible attribution and Volkswagen
    82–83
Polkinghorne, D. E. 30
polyphonic social media dialogue
    69, 71

positivist approach to sensemaking
    29–30
Postill, J. 85
poststructuralism 91
power in sensemaking 29–31, 92–95
Putnam, L. L. 2, 4, 8–9, 10, 11, 13, 17,
    40, 42, 72, 76, 102, 107
Puzzanghera, J. 82

Qaim, M. 99
Qiu, C. 58

Rainie, L. 71
Rao, J. M. 56
rationalization 67
Ravasi, D. 29
recontextualization 90
Reisigl, M. 88–89
resistance, discursive 94–95, 96, 101
retrospective sensemaking 25
Rheingold, H. 59
Rhodes, C. 30
Robichaud, D. 11–12
Rouse, J. 95
Ruel, S. 31
rules theory 33, 39–40

Saffer, A. J. 71
Sanders, B. 103
Save Darfur Facebook 87
Schenk, E. 57
Schoeneborn, D. 9, 10–13, 15, 17, 75
Seidl, D. 12, 47
sensemaking 1–2, 19–20; active
    authoring of events and frameworks
    in 24; authenticity and 43–45,
    105; collective 46, 86; cues in
    25–26, 39, 55–56, 100; discursive
    approach to 30, 67; enactment and
    (*see* enactment); establishing and/or
    maintaining routine 51; framing and
    13, 50–56, 110; human and non-
    human actants in 75–77; identity
    construction as component of
    24–26, 33–34; individual 91–92; as
    individual and psychological process
    91; language as substance of 23;
    legitimation and (*see* legitimation);
    limits of 67; literature on 27–29;
    noticing and bracketing in 74–75;
    as ongoing process 27, 93–94;
    order and disorder in 71–75;
    organizational crises and 73–74,

77; plausibility in (*see* plausibility); power within 29–31, 92–95; retrospective 25; rules theory and 33; shocks and junctures in 23–24; as social process 27; temporal 29, 106; Weickian 22–30, 33, 37; *see also* Critical Sensemaking (CSM) framework

Sergi, V. 45

Shirky, C. 86, 88

shocks and junctures in sensemaking 23–24

Situational Crisis Communication Theory 83

slacktivism 87–88

Smith, A. 71

Snapchat 106

Sniderman, P. 53

social activism 48–49, 59–65, 85–87; against Monsanto (*see* Monsanto); slactivism and 87–88; against Volkswagen (*see* Volkswagen)

social constructivism 1

social media networks and technologies: authenticity in 43–45; blocking of people on 71; communication as constitutive of organization (CCO) perspective and 19–20; Critical Sensemaking (CSM) and 4–5, 20; defining 2–3, 104–105; democratization through 49–50; digital democracy and 87; fragmentation and legitimation in 49–50; framing in 50–56; ideological segregation on 56; intertextuality in 88–89; legitimation within 67–69; methodology for studying organizational identity and (*see* discourse analysis methodology); volume of information from 1, 104

social process, sensemaking as 27

Social Systems Theory 11–12, 14

Stigliani, I. 29

Stohl, C. 85

storytelling, narrative 30

Sunstein, C. 50, 109

surveillance 93

Sutcliffe, K. 1–2

Sweetser, E. 50

Tamal, C. 98–99, 103

Taylor, J. R. 4–5, 9, 11–12, 17, 18, 58, 72, 107

Taylor, M. 49, 53, 70–71, 73, 108–109

temporal sensemaking 29, 106

text as physical artifact 19–20

textual agency 19–20

textual analysis *see* discourse analysis methodology

Theriault, S. 53

Thomas, J. 1, 24

Thorhauge, A. M. 19

Tienari, J. 67, 88

Townley, B. 110

Treem, J. W. 92–94

trending 101

Trittin, H. 75

Tsoukas, H. 15

Turkle, S. 20

Twitter 36, 45, 105–106; Monsanto and (*see* Monsanto); re-tweeting and Twitterstorms on 100–102; trending on 101; Volkswagen and (*see* Volkswagen)

Unger, J. W. 2, 37–38

Unger, R. 70

Vaara, E. 67, 88

validation, discursive 69

Vallee, J. 70

Van Dijk, T. A. 40

Van Every, E. J. 9, 17, 72, 107

Van Leeuwen, T. 67, 90

Vasquez, C. 9

Volkswagen 99; analysis of text and context on 81–82; apology by 83–84, *84*; background on 78–79; crisis communication by 80; dedicated hashtag and constrained range of possibilities in the conversation of 80; #dieselgate and 79–80, 96; influencers and context in communications on 80–81; plausible attribution and 82–83; 'two rogue engineers' at 83

warehouse expansion campaign 59–62

Weatherbee, T. G. 26

Weber, K. 25

Weick, K. E. 1–2, 5, 15, 22–30, 33, 37, 47, 105; on enactment of meaning 34; on faulty decisions 66; on individual script enactment 49; on micro-level actions created through

sensemaking 91; on noticing and bracketing 74–75; on organizational crises 73; on past experiences in sensemaking 54; on purpose of sensemaking as imposing order 71; on routines 51; on vocabulary of sensemaking 46
Westwood, S. J. 54–55
Wiebe, E. 29, 106
Winterkorn, M. 84
Wired 57

Wodak, R. 2, 67, 88–89, 90
Wood, R. 103
working out loud (WOL) 45, 105

Xenophon, N. 103

YouTube 19, 36

Zach, L. 75
Zaug, P. 9–11, 22, 64, 102
Zerfass, A. 5

For Product Safety Concerns and Information please contact our EU
representative GPSR@taylorandfrancis.com
Taylor & Francis Verlag GmbH, Kaufingerstraße 24, 80331 München, Germany